Jazz Play Trio

Fabulous Yellow Roman Candle

Straight Ahead

Blind Dancers

Jazz Play Trio

Fabulous Yellow Roman Candle Straight
Ahead
Blind Dancers

Charles Tidler

Ekstasis Editions

Canadian Cataloguing in Publication Data

Tidler, Charles
    Jazz Play Trio.

    Plays
    ISBN 1-896860-49-4

    I. Title.
    Ps8589.I34J39   1999   C812'.54   C99-911273-2
    PR9199.3.T497J39   1999

Cover Art: Michael Lewis
Author Photo: Frances Litman

Acknowledgements:
For *Fabulous Yellow Roman Candle*, the author wishes to thank The Canada Council for the Arts, CBC Radio Drama, and Chris Grayson.

Published in 1999 by:
Ekstasis Editions Canada Ltd.   **Ekstasis Editions**
Box 8474, Main Postal Outlet   Box 571,
Victoria, B.C. V8W 3S1   Banff, Alberta ToL oCo

THE CANADA COUNCIL | LE CONSEIL DES ARTS
FOR THE ARTS | DU CANADA
SINCE 1957 | DEPUIS 1957

Jazz Play Trio has been published with the assistance of a grant from the Canada Council and the Cultural Services Branch of British Columbia.

This book is for my Dad,
Bill Tidler.
He picks me up.

Contents

Three Jazz Plays:
An Introduction

When *Blind Dancers* first bruised its way on to the Toronto stage, in May 1981, the rallying cry was the jazz monologue. And that was a great thing to be writing, way back when. The language was sharp and vibrant, of course—as a playwright, Charles Tidler was already a brilliant poet. But there was something else, too, besides the language: the jazz ego was in there somewhere—front and centre, in fact, right at the edge of the stage. The player steps up to take his solo, insisting on the tune he heard so clearly in his own head... and insisting so persuasively, relying on his sometimes very private sense of pitch, leaning hard into the music and making that simple tune last forever... so that even the act of love was an act perpetually turning back on itself with a crazy glee. It's like the language itself—you can feel the exhilaration when you start taking out all those commas and periods, and it's a very personal thing too, because now that self-expression can keep flowing on forever. That was the jazz monologue.

It was more than ten years later that I had the profound delight of working with Charles on the stage premiere of *Fabulous Yellow Roman Candle*. And that's when I belatedly realized what Charles had probably always understood—that these weren't really monologues at all, they were really dialogues. They were dialogues between poet and horn player, between actor and musician, between words and music.

I think the night when I came to know that simple fact was the night when Todd Duckworth discovered he could play a perfect duet with Victor Bateman... Todd playing his belly with his fists while Victor played his big stand-up bass. They played together every night after that, at the same moment in the evening, Todd crashing over to Victor in a kind of a panic, like someone who really, really needed to be there. And it was a small duet that always worked, the music unleashing a tumult of child-like energy which could carry an audience along without reservations to an unknown destination.

Every night, in *Fabulous Yellow Roman Candle*, the actors and the musicians found new and more unlikely ways to work together on the solos, sometimes way out in left field and always far beyond the simple challenge of you show me/I'll show you. When you release an actor into the idea of song and rhythm, the results can be just as wonderfully unpredictable as when you release a musician into the idea of poetry. The actors found more and more amazing ways to sing, sometimes without even raising their voices, and the band found new and extraordinary things they could say as they wrapped their improv around the text. And on the best nights, the encounter of words and music was pure magic.

Later, when I thought about it, I realized that there was another kind of dialogue going on here, too... a dialogue between Charles and him/self on the subject of creativity and inertia, fame and drunkenness, perpetual motion and living death. The music was a place for meditation.

Fabulous Yellow Roman Candle is a play about Kerouac, of course, but it's also a play about Charles Tidler. And his view of Kerouac may be roughly accurate, but it's expressed with such a deep subjectivity that it propels the work out of the realm of hagiography into the realm of pure poetry.

And all that jazz is an especially good place for meditation, because the mind can wander as it will, but those thoughts are always cradled in the pocket of the rhythm or in the key of the music... so you can sit inside the same muse for a long time without starting to get impatient. And that's especially true in the modal varieties of jazz where the notes come fast in a sliding scale of perfect geometry, careening wildly and sometimes even falling like sheets of rain (as someone once said about Coltrane), but always revolving around some virtual centre of a perfect pitch that remains somehow mysterious. There's no doubt about it, you can always hear better when the music's playing.

And that makes for another kind of dialogue again, a dialogue between Charles and his own half-crazed god. Perhaps that's why, on the nights the music was good, I always remember Charles standing crooked by the side of the stage, his head lifting sideways and his glasses askew, with that crazy grin spreading helplessly across his face, as the music starts to play.

Bill Lane, Toronto
September 9, 1999

Fabulous Yellow Roman Candle

A bebop hagiography

"What can one man do for another? What can a man do for his brother? What can a man do for love? Nothing. Nothing."
— Lucien Carr

Fabulous Yellow Roman Candle was first produced by New Theatre Projects as part of the Toronto duMaurier Jazz Festival at Theatre Passe Muraille, June 22- July 4, 1993, in Toronto, Ontario. Directed by Bill Lane. Produced by Jain Dickson. Designed by Jim Plaxton. Music composed by Nic Gotham. The stage manager was Kim Ritchie.

Cast:

JACK KEROUAC	Ron White
GABRIELLE	Jacqueline Blais
NEAL, MALCOLM, BLACKIE, GUY	Todd Duckworth

Trio:

SAXOPHONE	Nic Gotham
STANDUP BASS	Victor Bateman
DRUMS	Howard Gaul

Players:

JACK KEROUAC, about 35, a writer.
NEAL, 30s, Jack's best friend.
GABRIELLE, about 65, Jack's mother.
MALCOLM, 40s, a New York editor.
BLACKIE, 60s, a muleskinner.
GUY-IN-A-SUIT, grey flannel.

NEAL, MALCOLM, BLACKIE and GUY are played by the same actor.

Time:

Summer 1956 to New Years Eve 1957.

Place:

New York City; Florida; North Carolina; California; The High Cascades; Heaven.

Musicians:

Bebop trio — drums, bass, sax.

Set: A small jazz club, circa 1950s, slowly bleeds from upstage right through downstage right into a tenement apartment downstage left and upstage left. Downstage right there is a small table and two chairs for the club. Upstage right there is a stage large enough for a trio plus a high stool behind a standing microphone. Upstage left there is a tenement kitchen, sink, cupboards, shelves, table and chairs. There is a huge fluorescent crucifix hanging from the wall. Downstage left there is an old stuffed armchair in front of a large T.V. Upstage center there must be a high space which is neither jazz club nor tenement apartment. This is the High Cascades. It also serves as a bridge from time to time between the layers of worlds of illusion. Here all is exposed bythe trickery, the transience, the pretense of the theatre. Here, if only for the winking of an eye, the real world is the live stage.

Lighting: Theatrical and unreal. The jazz club is dark, smoky, draped. There is a spot on the stool. Also a spot in the high space upstage center. Though realistic in intent, the tenement apartment should be lit somewhat theatrically.

Music: Charlie Parker-inspired spontaneous bop composition. This is also a note for much of the language of the play.

Scene One.

The Village Vanguard. New York City. New Years Eve, 1957.

As a preshow, the jazz trio has been warming up, two or three numbers —"Straight, No Chaser" by Thelonious Monk is a suggestion. At one of the tables in the club, JACK KEROUAC sleeps dead drunk to the world. He is dressed in a flannel checked shirt, sports jacket, chinos, loafers, no socks. Despite his present condition, he is a handsome man. He carries a large aspirin bottle full of cheap bourbon. As the houselights dim and the stage lights come up on the jazz club, the trio is playing a version of Cole Porter's "I Love You," and Jack begins to stir at his table. We can sort of make out with a bit of effort what he has to say.

JACK: Where am I? ... I can't do this ... What am I doing here? ... Who the fuck do you think you are? Jack Kerouac? (Laughs) ... No, no, no, can't do, won't do this ... Don't even know my lines ... Jack be nimble, Jack be quick, Jack went splat like a lenten fart over the candle stick ... Are you a man or a mouse? ... Mousey ... Mousey ... Mousey, mousey, mousey, mousey, mousey, mousey, mousey ...

          (Lights up on NEAL in the High Cascades. Casual and confi-
          dent, he wears jeans, boots, but no shirt.)
NEAL: Hey, Jack.

JACK: Neal.

NEAL: You remember the night we picked up that funny little fat queer travelling salesman?
          (Neal swoops down from the mountain.)
Broken cardboard suitcase bursting cornucopia mother's little helper greenie weenie diet pills snappy Harry S. Truman fedora fifty dollar double-breasted blue pinstripe suit hitchhiking on a straight stretch of dark grey gloom highway ribbon just outside of Sioux City, Iowa ... there we were the three of us side by side on the wide plush pile front seat of that brand new showroom '49 Hudson me at the wheel you riding

15

ing shotgun funny little fat queer in the middle crossing the whole state of Iowa plowing the long night furrow black like a spring field all the way to the Mississippi River ... and when we hit it I think it was Mingus yeah it was Mingus standup bass solo bop bop bebop on the radio the stars lighting up the sky like buttons on a jukebox enough butter in the full moon for all the pop corn in Kansas ... when we hit it that two lane bridge of American steel uniting east and west the cowboy to the skyscraper 85 miles an hour flying into a new dawn he had me in his left hand and you in his right hand ... and we all came together vroom! (Short pause) Member that, Jack?

JACK: Gerard est mort.

NEAL: You should of put that in your book.
                (Neal laughs. He exits. Lights fade. End of scene.)

Scene Two.

A small apartment. Orlando Florida. New Years Eve 1957.

(GABRIELLE sits in the armchair lit by the glow of the T.V. In her arms and on her lap she cradles a dead tabby cat recently run over by a passing car. She dresses simply and neatly, an overproud French Canadian matron a bit gone to seed thanks to alcohol and years of transient poverty. She clings tenacious as a bulldog to her belief in Catholicism and the memory of her first son, Gerard, who died a saint at the age of nine in 1926. Here she is deeply moaning. The cat's name is Tyke, but she says it like 'teak'.)

GABRIELLE: Teak ... Teak ... Teak ... Teak ... Teak ... Teak ... Teak ... Teak ... Teak ...
          (Lights up on Jack.)

JACK: Gerard est mort. (Short pause) We all die, Mama.

GABRIELLE: Good, damn it, good.
          (Lights down on Gabrielle. End of scene.)

Scene Three.

Jazz club. New Years Eve, 1957.

(Lights up on the trio. They close out "I Love You". Whatever applause. THE SAX PLAYER steps up to the mike.)

SAX PLAYER: Thank you.
        (Pause)
Now I'd like to introduce to you ... the novelist Jack Kerouac.

JACK: Help me.
        (Sax Player helps Jack. Finally, he's sitting on the stool at the mike.)
Welcome ... welcome to New York City, the Big Apple, New Years Eve, 1957 ... the Village Vanguard wishes to announce the opening of new sessions and new feelings, daddy-o ... with Jack Kerouac, the King of the Beats, just call me Jack ... we're going to open with a little *On The Road* asphalt bebop, man ... I call this number "Frisco To The Apple" ... hit it, boys ...
        (Jack unfolds a roadmap of America. The trio improvs with Jack who sings, chants, scats.)
San Francisco ... Oakland ... Berkeley ... Dixon ... Davis ... Sacramento ... Roseville ... Truckee ... Reno, Nevada ... Sparks ... Loverock ... Winnemucca ... Battle Mountain ... Elko ... Wells ... Wendover, Utah ... Grantsville ... Murray ... Salt Lake City ... Coalville ... Evanston, Wyoming ... Lyman ... Granger ... Green River ... Rock Springs ... Parco ... Hanna ...
        (The trio in transition.)
Begin not, O Muse of Eisenhower America T.V. America mushroom cloud dream of suburban backyard barbecue America, begin not with Walt Disney Hollywood image but deep dive into the depths of the belly swim in that sea reclaim the jewel of language ... begin with a mouse on a mountaintop crying for a vision of meatwheel compassion ... oh saxophone word snare drum mind ... begin with me ... hey, I'm a mouse not a man ... begin with me, Jack Kerouac, Beat Generation novelist subterranean hobo dharma bum highway clown ghostly

nightmare visionary mouse ... begin in tenement textile town Lowell, Massachusetts ... begin March 12, 1922 ... Oh mama mama mama ... Oh oh oh here I am Jean-Louis ... Ti-Jean ... just call me Jack ... my father worked at the printing trade my mother operated the dye vat in the shoeplant ... begin with beautiful childhood roaming fields and woods and riverbanks ... begin with poor little sickly Saint Gerard my brother lover of kittens birds bugs dogs mice who died at the age of nine when I was four ... how can I go on after that what am I doing here? ... begin with the great evil snake wants to swallow all human-kindness shit out our souls nightmare visions oblivion lost gone sad ghostly stars beating like moths against the milky way lightbulb of God's eternal love ... begin with college football hero Columbia 1940 ... begin with the war heroic kitchen scullion of merchant ships ... begin with girl sex boy sex booze drugs high on poetry and Charlie Parker bebop mind juice body meat nonstop talk William Burroughs Allen Ginsberg Neal Cassidy insane reality ... begin with the road to Chicago Denver New Orleans San Francisco where the Beat Genera-tion danced the two lane ribbon of asphalt ... and I followed behind like I always do following everybody down the road ... Medicine Bow ... Laramie ... Cheyenne ... Pine Bluff ... Kimball, Nebraska ... Potter ... Chappell ... Big Spring ... Ogallala ... North Platte ... Grand Island ... Central City ... North Bend ... Wakefield ... Sioux City, Iowa.

> (The trio stops playing. The stage goes black except for a spot on Jack who looks tiny and far away.)

Neal? ...Mousey? ... Gerard?

> (End of scene.)

Scene Four.

A small apartment. Rocky Mount, N.C. Summer, 1956.

(Lights up. Jack crosses the stage.)

JACK: Begin, begin, begin ... summer 1956. I'm visiting my mother for a few weeks redbrick walkup a little apartment in Rocky Mount, North Carolina, where the stars in the sky so close you can smell them, and the lilacs, and all that homecooking only my dearest mom knows how to do.
> (Lights up on Gabrielle who is busily and noisily removing dishes and pots and pans and silverware from shelves and cupboards and depositing them in the sink. MALCOLM sits on the edge of a chair at the table. He dresses casually like a professor on holiday, cotton shirt with an open collar, roomy jacket, black shoes, an old leather briefcase. He feels out of place and pressed for time. Jack falls back into the armchair. He is drunkenly singing.)

"He was just a wayward angel falling through the sky ... He was just a wayward angel falling." (Stops singing.) Malcolm.

MALCOLM: Jack

JACK: What's the response?

Malcolm: Response ... to what?

JACK: Blues. There's a call line. Then there's repeat line. Then ... response.

GABRIELLE: You got a problem.

JACK: Problem.

GABRIELLE: A drinking problem.

JACK: Suppose you don't. (Short pause) Malcolm.

Malcolm: Jack.

JACK: What's response?

MALCOLM: "Lord, have mercy on his soul."

GABRIELLE: Every dish in the house ... filthy.

JACK: Joyce did the dishes, mom.

GABRIELLE: Don't speak that woman's name in my house.

JACK: I sat here and watched her ... every dish, glass, pot, pan.

GABRIELLE: The women you bring home.

JACK: In this chair.

GABRIELLE: Jewish princess in a packsack.

JACK: Careful.

GABRIELLE: What?

JACK: Malcolm's Jewish.

MALCOLM: Jack.

GABRIELLE: You a Jew?

MALCOLM: I'm afraid Jack's mistaken, ma'am. My family's all Methodist.

GABRIELLE: (To Jack) Liar.

JACK: I told Joyce everything.

GABRIELLE: Glad she's gone.

JACK: How you like to do the pots soak them in hot soapy water and do the glasses first so they shine in your hand like an empty rainbow.

GABRIELLE: She didn't use my Joy.

JACK: She used the soap that was under the sink.

GABRIELLE: Laundry detergent.

JACK: Dish soap.

GABRIELLE: You can fool all the people some time, and some of the people all time ... but you can't fool mom.

JACK: (With Gabrielle) ... but you can't fool mom.

GABRIELLE: I always use my Joy.

JACK: (Sings) "He was just a wayward angel falling through the sky"...

GABRIELLE: Stay out of my whiskey. There's a mark.

JACK: Where you going?

GABRIELLE: Down to the store with your poor mother's last few pennies to buy a bottle of my Joy.

JACK: I thought you were going to make Malcolm here a cup of tea.

GABRIELLE: I'm not making tea in a filthy teapot.

JACK: Go to the store. Go straight to Hell for all I care.

MALCOLM: Missus Kerouac, please, don't go out of your way on my account. I can't stay, really, I'm sorry.

GABRIELLE: You're such a nice man, educated, too, with the manners of a gentleman. Bet you never talk like that to your mother.

MALCOLM: Mothers are the backbone of America, Missus Kerouac.

GABRIELLE: You're so sweet. Can't you talk some sense into him?

MALCOLM: Well, I'd like to try.

GABRIELLE: I pray every day to the memory of my dead son Saint Gerard that Jackie will listen to me.

JACK: Listen to you all the time.

GABRIELLE: But he hasn't listened to a word I've said since the day we laid the body of his dead father in the ground, and he swore on his father's deathbed that he would always listen to his mother.

JACK: I listen to you.

GABRIELLE: On your father's last dying breath you swore to Saint Gerard.

JACK: Yeah, that I would always take care of you. I do.

GABRIELLE: Sure you do.

JACK: I do. When my first book came out I even bought you a brand new Motorola.

GABRIELLE: Where is it? Broke.

JACK: You've got another T.V. now.
GABRIELLE: You've disgraced your father's memory.

JACK: It's not fair for you to say that. (Short pause) Mama ...

GABRIELLE: (To Malcolm) If Jackie doesn't get his next advance for the new book I don't know what I'll boil up for supper tonight, air I guess.

MALCOLM: Please don't worry about Jack's advance, Missus Kerouac. I'm going to write him a check.

GABRIELLE: When?

MALCOLM: I'll get my checkbook.

GABRIELLE: One hundred dollars?

MALCOLM: One hundred dollars.

GABRIELLE: Write it in my name.

MALCOLM: Jack?

JACK: Write it in her name.

GABRIELLE: Gabrielle Kerouac ... two l's.

MALCOLM: Here you go, Missus Kerouac.

GABRIELLE: One hundred dollars.

JACK: Proof. I did not disgrace my father's memory.

GABRIELLE: I'm going to the store to buy my Joy. You listen to this nice man, Jackie.

MALCOLM: It's been a pleasure meeting you, Missus Kerouac.

(Jack roars like a lion. Gabrielle exits.)
JACK: (Laughs) That's what my father always used to do ... roar like a lion. Works every time.

MALCOLM: Can we talk now, Jack?

JACK: Just a minute. I'm looking for something.

MALCOLM: My wife and kids are waiting in the car.

JACK: Tell them to come on in.

MALCOLM: You don't want three kids in here.

JACK: Sure I do. Go get them. They can play with the cat. Tyke likes kids.

MALCOLM: Jack, I haven't got that kind of time. I woke up in Florida this morning, and I want to sleep in Virginia tonight. I have to get back to New York before the family dog and I come to blows.

JACK: (Finds a bottle) Jackpot. Hold out on me. Some fox. See? See the line? She's got it marked with black crayon so I don't take any. What kind of mother would do that? (Pours a big drink.) Drink?

MALCOLM: I can't.

JACK: Drink.

MALCOLM: No, Jack.

JACK: You don't love me if you won't drink with me.

MALCOLM: I love you, Jack, but I can't go back to my car all liquored up.

JACK: Okay.

MALCOLM: Can we talk now about this Seattle business?

JACK: Watch this an old trick I learned in the Merchant Marine I call it walking down the line. See, you smudge out the old crayon line with your thumb then mark the new line with the smudge. Look at it now.

MALCOLM: Looks like someone smudged up your mother's line.

JACK: No, it doesn't.
          (Jack rehides the bottle.)

MALCOLM: Talk to me.

JACK: I can't offer you anything but oblivion.

MALCOLM: What the hell are you doing going to Seattle?

JACK: What I'm talking about.

MALCOLM: I thought you were coming to New York next week.

JACK: Naw naw I need solitude dream drift with the clouds stop the brain machinery. I want to climb to heaven where my brother lives Saint Gerard amid the Pooh Bear stars.

MALCOLM: Talk sense.

JACK: All I talk. You want it straight?

MALCOLM: Please.

JACK: I got a job with the U.S. Agriculture Department as a fire lookout in the Mount Baker National Forest.

MALCOLM: Okay.

JACK: The High Cascades.

MALCOLM: Allright.

JACK: Desolation Ridge ... icicle for a backbone brrrr makes me shiver.

MALCOLM: I get the picture. Now you give me one minute.

JACK: Shoot.

MALCOLM: New York thinks this Beat Generation thing is really going to take off. I keep telling them you're the guy they want, Jack Kerouac, the King of the Beats.

JACK: I'm not a king I'm a mouse going up into the mountains to cry for a vision.

MALCOLM: They want to publish *On The Road.*
    (Pause)
Do you hear me?
    (Pause)
We want to do it now, if, Jack, if, if you'll consent to make a few changes.

JACK: Changes ...

MALCOLM: The prose doesn't bother me, it's the structure of the book.
    (Pause)
The structure it fractures ... too much crossing back and forth across the continent.

JACK: That's the way it happened.

MALCOLM: Back and forth, back and forth like a pendulum. Needs cuts, Jack. Some events need consolidation. You don't always need another car ride to tell the story.
    (Pause)
You hear what I'm saying?

JACK: I wrote that book in three weeks of spontaneous bop composition on a hundred and twenty-five foot roll of paper.

MALCOLM: So?

JACK: So I can't change it. That's the way I did it.

MALCOLM: Seven years ago, and nobody will touch it.

(Pause)
JACK: What changes?

(Malcolm digs for a sheet of paper in his briefcase.)
MALCOLM: Specifically ... condense the trip to New Orleans, omit the bus trip from San Francisco to New York via the northwest, condense the trip from Denver to San Francisco, omit Sal's visit with the first wife in Detroit, and I insist, I insist you delete that paragraph which explicitly describes Dean Moriarty's relations with the homosexual you pick up hitchhiking outside of Denver.

JACK: Sioux City.

MALCOLM: Sioux City?

JACK: Where it happened ... really happened.

MALCOLM: Whatever. Doesn't matter. Cut it. (Short pause) That's about it, not a lot of work. A little realignment ... here and there a few careful cuts. (Short pause) Nobody writes perfectly the first draft. We're not God.

JACK: Sure we are.

MALCOLM: *On The Road* is a great book, and it's going to hit the bookstores like a bombshell. You're going to be famous, Jack.

JACK: Isn't it true that you come into the world a sweet child believing in everything under your father's roof. Be a football hero. Be the President. Be Shakespeare. (Short pause) Then comes the day when you know you are wretched and miserable and poor and blind and naked. Vanity.

(Pause)

MALCOLM: You're a hard guy to deal with, Jack. Look, at least promise me, before you take off for Seattle, that you'll write me a letter in which you address the problem of the re-writes. You've got to give New York that much. Okay?
  (Pause. Jack sort of nods.)
Okay. I gotta run.

JACK: What is that feeling when you're driving away from people and they recede until all you can see is the vanishing point?

MALCOLM: Keep in touch. Goodby, Jack.
  (Malcolm exits. Pause.)

JACK: The feeling is goodby.
  (Lights down. End of scene.)

Scene Five.

The same. A few days later.

(Jack stands in the middle of the apartment. He's trying on a new pair of chinos of which the legs are too long. Gabrielle is at his feet on her hands and knees. She is securing the hemline with little pins which she takes from her mouth. On the kitchen table there is a box of jelly donuts, whisky bottle, and a portable typewriter. By the T.V. is a big backpack in the process of being packed for the road.)

GABRIELLE: Reste tranquil.

JACK: I don't want you crawling around at my feet.

GABRIELLE: Bouge-pas.

JACK: Ow.

GABRIELLE: Don't slouch.

JACK: How long is this going to take?

GABRIELLE: If you don't hold still I'll never get it right.

JACK: Right enough for a mountain I reckon.

GABRIELLE: Stay off the sauce up there, Jackie.

JACK: That's my plan.

GABRIELLE: I don't want you falling off any mountain.

JACK: You can't fall off a mountain.

GABRIELLE: And don't have anything to do with your crazy friends when you're going through San Francisco. Don't even call them up.

JACK: Ah, Ma, you'd like some of them.

GABRIELLE: They always get you into trouble.

JACK: No, they don't.

GABRIELLE: Stay away from those people, especially that Neal Cassidy. (Short pause) Jackie.

JACK: I will. I promise.

GABRIELLE: Swear by Saint Gerard.

JACK: I swear by Saint Gerard.

GABRIELLE: Hold still.

JACK: I am.

GABRIELLE: Bon.

JACK: Can I move now?

GABRIELLE: Take the pant off.
          (Jack takes the pants off.)
Underwear. Filthy.

JACK: Don't do that.

GABRIELLE: I guess you got nothing I ain't seen before. You were in diaper until you were three.
          (Jack puts on his other pair of pants.)
Just a minute. I got you a little present.
          (Gabrielle has a shopping bag.)

JACK: What is it?

GABRIELLE: Look.

JACK: Wow, what beautiful shirts.
          (The bag contains six brand-new shirts identical to the one
          Jack is wearing.)
All my favorite.

GABRIELLE: Well, let's see if they fit.

JACK: I love the big pockets on these shirts. When I worked as a
brakeman on the railroad I carried my brakeman's manual in my
breast pocket right here. Fits great.

GABRIELLE: And I got you six pair of sock and six pair of underwear.

JACK: I bet you bought all these new clothes with your coffee can
money didn't you?

GABRIELLE: The shirt were on sale three ninety-five at Woolworth's.

JACK: You're my gal, Ma, you're my number one girl.

GABRIELLE: Let me hem your pants while you write your letter to
New York.

JACK: Ah, you never let me hug you, Ma.

GABRIELLE: Write your letter.
          (Gabrielle sits in the armchair and hems the pants by hand.
          Her stitches are strong, sewn with professional authority. Jack
          takes forever to get to the typewriter. Finally, he sits down at
          the table. Long pause. Jack strikes a single key. Pause.)

JACK: I can't do this.

GABRIELLE: Have another jelly donut, Jackie. Sugar's good for the thinker.

JACK: I can't rewrite my book any more than I can tell a lie. It happened the way it happened. The whole thing is the truth.

GABRIELLE: Mon dieu, the fuss you make over a dirty book.

JACK: They want me to cut it, rewrite, edit. May as well take a sharp knife to a set of tires on a brand-new Hudson.
(Pause)
I won't change a word.

GABRIELLE: What are you going to do up on your mountain then, sit around mumbling Buddha mumbo jumbo? That stuff never made you a dime.

JACK: I want to go up there on the mountain and talk to Gerard.

GABRIELLE: Gerard's not going to talk to you after you abandon your mother to the poor house.

JACK: I want to change places with him in heaven.

GABRIELLE: (Laughs) Voyons donc. God would trade one of his saint for the like of you? You got another thing coming if you think that.

JACK: But if Gerard and I traded places you'd be happy, Mama. Gerard would be alive again, sweet Saint Gerard alive. You could have the son you always wanted.

GABRIELLE: (Laughs) And you would be the new saint, hein?

JACK: Mama, I just want to stop living with an open grave.

    (Pause)
GABRIELLE: Gerard is the saint in this family. (Short pause) Seigneur, may your brother Saint Gerard forgive me, but one saint is plenty enough for any family to have to suffer through. (Short pause) He was my innocent little boy, only nine years old, Jackie, and he was sick, so

sick and on his deathbed for over two year. I begged God, "Take me, take me, don't take my innocent little baby. Take me, take me." (Short pause) I remember the day he died.

JACK: "Gerard est mort!"

GABRIELLE: I'll never forgive you for that, Jackie.

JACK: I was four years old.

GABRIELLE: That's no excuse.

JACK: The day Gerard died, I was happy because I thought our family would be happy again like it was before Gerard got sick.

GABRIELLE: The day Gerard died, I knew it would be that day, sometime in the afternoon, I knew that morning, I was in the kitchen making breakfast Gerard's favorite boiling oatmeal and raisins, and I remember stepping out onto the January backporch doorstep to scrape some frozen sour cream into the cat's dish, and the cold hit me like sheet of glass breaking into my face. I heard little snap like an icicle snap and then I heard the strangest thing a little cry low as a mouse. I think it was an angel singing. And then it stopped, like that, no sound, nothing, just me and the cold, and I knew.

JACK: The day Gerard died, I remember the nuns coming to our house like a line of crows crossing sun on snow.

GABRIELLE: The day Gerard died, my heart froze up, and I swallowed it whole. (Short pause) And your papa, your papa, the beast ... Leo was no use to me at all, storming around the house like a brute, an ape, drinking, shaking his hairy fist at the crucifix, bellowing blasphemy, "Go on, God, get out of my house, don't call yourself God in my house." Oh, the beast, the beast. I said "Leo, Leo, you can't fight God, you'll never win." And your papa, your papa said, "I'm not fighting, Gabrielle, I'm, I'm dying." (Short pause) Little sliver pieces of my heart have been curdling in my stomach for thirty years.

34

JACK: I remember the black-cowled nuns filing one by one into Gerard's bedroom to hear firsthand the little stories of his sainthood.

GABRIELLE: Yes. The Mother Superior recorded it word for word with a little gold pencil into a large leather notebook embossed in goldleaf with the title *Visions of Gerard.*

JACK: There's the miracle of the little starving sparrow.

GABRIELLE: The vision of la Sainte-Vierge in the schoolyard.

JACK: "Heaven is the earth, and the earth is Heaven, but we don't know it yet" is what the Madonna said to him, her exact words.

GABRIELLE: And la Sainte-Vierge flooded the schoolyard with a shower of roses. (Short pause) Tender child.

JACK: My favorite is Gerard and the mouse.

GABRIELLE: And the cat.

JACK: The day Gerard found the mouse he was walking home from school and I'd run all the way to the schoolyard to meet him I'd lost my ear muffs playing army in the woods that morning and it was cold I had to run with my mittens over my ears. I remember Gerard was shivering like a skinned rabbit, stamping up and down on the balls of his feet trying to hide from the cold in his little cloth coat.

GABRIELLE: Jackie, believe me, it was all I could afford after your father's card games and liquor.

JACK: The cold was in both of us, so we took a shortcut home down the alley behind the greengrocer's store and there between two oily cardboard boxes of frozen rotting vegetables Gerard saw a little mouse squeaking caught it's left front foreleg crushed in a mousetrap. "Hello, little mouse," said Gerard. "Don't be afraid, let me help you." And Gerard carefully tenderly released the little steel bar on the trapspring

35

from the mouse's foreleg, and Gerard carried the mouse in the bottom of his toque like a little bird in a nest all the way home.

GABRIELLE: Gerard was bare-headed in the cold?

JACK: Yes, Mama, don't you remember?

GABRIELLE: Ben trop.

JACK: Gerard carried the mouse home and he built it a little bed out of a cigar box and an old faded-blue dish towel and fed it cow's milk from a little eyedropper and made a little splint out of a popsickle stick and pieces of old string ah the tenderness of Saint Gerard.

GABRIELLE: La tendresse.

JACK: His little fingers tying the tiny little knots. Gerard loved the little mouse a pure and simple love even I four year-old stumbler over words and staircases even I could read the love like light around his face little Gerard looking after the little mouse.

GABRIELLE: And the next day the cat ate it.

JACK: Gerard was sick to his heart, but he didn't get mad at the cat or treat it mean.

GABRIELLE: He gave the cat a sermon.

JACK: It is recorded in gold pencil by the venerable nuns of Lowell, Mass., that Saint Gerard delivered a sermon to the cat on compassion, the art of sad understanding with all sentient creatures.

GABRIELLE: And the cat listened to the whole thing.

        (Pause)
JACK: What are we ever going to do, Mama? What's to become of us?

36

GABRIELLE: Write that letter to New York and tell them you'll change the book any way they like it.

JACK: I don't think I can do that.

GABRIELLE: Jackie, you're the only man I got left. Me, I need a breadwinner now not a saint, somebody to look after me in my old age. Your book is a chance to make us somebody important with lots of money, somebody in America, somebody more than the pain of being the mother of Saint Gerard.

JACK: But you said it was a dirty book.

GABRIELLE: Dirty smirty, je m'en fou. Let the dirty people read it. I'll spend their money anyway.
      (Jack laughs.)
Jackie. Listen to your mother.

JACK: I am.

GABRIELLE: Go to your mountain if you have to go and do whatever it is you have to do up there.

JACK: Okay.

GABRIELLE: But promise, promise me that you'll work on your book up there, and whatever New York wants, New York gets. (Short pause) Will you do that ... for your memere who loves you more than I can ever tell?

JACK: I will ... and swear by Saint Gerard.

GABRIELLE: That's my boy.
      (Gabrielle hugs Jack.)

JACK: Yeah, and if the book's a bestseller like Malcolm says, maybe we can even buy a house out on Long Island somewhere Walt Whitman Paumanok country, a big house your dream house, Mama, with a view of the endless blue sea the endless blue sky and the house will have an extra special room blessed by the kiss of the sacred sisters, a room to be a shrine to the memory of St. Gerard, and even a room for Papa, too.

GABRIELLE: That would be nice.
        (Pause)
Bon b'en, rien ici, lazy puss, let's try these pant on now.

JACK: Golly, Ma, I don't want to try the pants on now. I already got pants on.

GABRIELLE: Voyons, voyons, you got nothing I ain't seen before.

JACK: We already know they fit. I'll try them on later.

GABRIELLE: You'll try them on now.

JACK: Mama, no.
            (Lights down. End of scene.)

Scene Six.

Jazz club. A dream scene.

(Lights up on the trio. Neal is with them. Jack enters, and Neal snaps out a fifty-dollar bill.)

NEAL: Fifty bucks.

JACK: What? I can't.

NEAL: Pay me back. (Laughs) When you're famous.

          (Jack takes the bill.)
JACK: I hate this.

NEAL: I love you, man.

JACK: No, you can't, you don't want to do that.

NEAL: Carve your initials into my arm with a stolen car key prove it to you, Jack.

JACK: I hate myself.

NEAL: You're just beat. Fuck, come on, give me a hug.
          (They hug and kiss. The trio begins to play, and Neal and Jack launch into a scat duet.)
          By golly but a guy does got to go goofing ...

JACK: Ever now and then ...

NEAL: Down ...

JACK: To the Pacific Ocean eat a fish ...

NEAL: Over coals ...

JACK: Beneath the stars ...

NEAL: Stars talk to people drink a little wine ...

JACK: And beer ...

NEAL: Smoke pot ...

JACK: Fall in love ...

NEAL: Wouldn't that be a grand and fine ...

JACK: Fine ...

NEAL: Delicious folly ...

JACK: The record player precarious in the open window ...

NEAL: Bebops the lonely loon bay ...

JACK: Everybody goofing poetry and come what may ...

NEAL: Maybe even girls ...

JACK: Girls well yeah ...

NEAL: I like to just lean like this against the kitchen counter ...

JACK: Cause I'm closer to the moth-spun light and ...

NEAL: All the food and booze ...

JACK: The fridge ...

NEAL: The stove ...

JACK: The sink ...

NEAL: The toilet's not too far away and ...

JACK: Most of all ...

NEAL / JACK: The women ...

JACK: Each a unique vision of ...

NEAL: Woman ...

JACK: Kind ...

NEAL: Always hang out passing through ...

JACK: Goofing with food and babes and ...

NEAL: I lean on the kitchen counter with drink in hand ...

JACK: Hanging around the kitchen ...

NEAL: The ladies seem to like that ...

JACK: Think I'm probably ...

NEAL / JACK: Domestic ...

JACK: Hanging goofy in the kitchen like that ...

NEAL: And none of them seem to care or mind ...

JACK: I got no job no house ...

NEAL: No car ...

JACK: Nothing but a packsack of haiku and ancient sorrow ...

NEAL: The women in the kitchen ...

(Neal exits.)

JACK: Don't care about that because I look good to them a man goofing in the kitchen is a kind of pleasant peace all is well between a man and about any woman who passes through.

> (The trio stops playing. Jack looks around.)

Neal?

> (Pause. Jack gets up on the stool at the mike. The trio begins to play.)

Begin begin begin ... begin in San Francisco Greyhound bus station hum hear that lonesome diesel engine drum ... begin in Sausalito ... Santa Rosa ... Eureka ... Cresent City ... Grant's Pass ... Roseburg ... Salem ... Mount Angel ... Gladstone ... Portland ... Kelso ... Castle Rock ... Olympia ... Tacoma .... begin in Seattle totem-poles fishboats cannery sheds ancient locomotives boxcars ...

> (The trio in transition. Jack gets up from the stool, and with mike in hand, begins to wander.)

Begin to hitchhike old Highway 99 ... begin the High Cascades ... begin to climb the great white heart of heaped and twisted mountain rock ... begin to climb to the end of the world ... begin to climb into high Heaven where my brother lives Saint Gerard.

> (Jack begins to climb the mountain. Meanwhile, BLACKIE enters and sits down at the table in the night club. He's dressed like a mountainman, heavy coat, old floppy hat. He pulls out a deck of cards.)

Begin below Ross Lake, Ross Dam, climb a thousand feet. This is the day, rainy morning, I meet my first muleskinner, an old mountain-man named Blackie Burns ... my guide to the tiny cabin up on top of Desolation Peak.

> (Blackie is playing a game of Solitaire.)

BLACKIE: Never heard of the name Caraway before.

JACK: Kerouac. It's French Canadian, an old Breton name. The motto on the coat of arms is "Love, work, and suffer."

BLACKIE: (Laughs) I'm going to put you where nobody can reach

42

you, and you're going to suffer ... plenty.

JACK: Yeah, I'm looking forward to it.

BLACKIE: Sixty-three days and nights of complete solitude in the wilderness.

JACK: How many people in this day and age get a chance to do that?

BLACKIE: You bring along any brandy?

JACK: Naw, I'm off the sauce on account of my dear old mother. I'm a writer. I'm going up there to work on a novel I'm trying to get published in New York.

BLACKIE: You're gonna wushed you had a drink around if the Sasquatch comes knocking on your door.

JACK: What's a Sasquatch?
        (The sax reacts to the line. Jack climbs.)
The trail rises steeply. We climb. Another thousand feet.

BLACKIE: See it?

JACK: What?

BLACKIE: The mountaintop, see it?

JACK: I don't know.

BLACKIE: Soon's we get up high as that we're almost there.

JACK: Now, I see it.
        (Jack climbs.)
Again we climb, yet another thousand feet wind sleet snow the world blind stinging white.

BLACKIE: There she is.

JACK: Where?

BLACKIE: There.

JACK: That's my cabin? That shack?

BLACKIE: Welcome to Desolation.
            (Jack is on the mountaintop.)

JACK: What a miserable hole this place is, cold, dirty, leftover groceries everywhere, mud, magazines torn to shreds.

BLACKIE: Rats or mice.

JACK: You're starting a fire?

BLACKIE: Cold enough, ain't it?

JACK: I can't live here.

BLACKIE: Go unpack some of your coffee and spam and powdered eggs, and I'll start cleaning up in here. No use bellyaching.

            (Jack opens an imaginary door.)
JACK: Creakkk ... I step outside, cup my hands to the wind and sleet and snow. (Yells) What is the meaning of the void?
            (The trio in transition. Blackie exits.)
Begin with a scardey-pants with pants down hole in jeans and mind fat with vanity mouse on a mountaintop questioning wind sleet snow the void answers with silence.
            (Beat of silence.)
Up on that mountain I went crazy. Two months alone nobody to talk to nobody but the rangers on the crackly two-way radio nobody really two months solitary stone cold alone in the doom doomy doomiest gloom void ... thinking about *On The Road* famous ... thinking about

44

Saint Gerard and famous ... thinking about mama and oblivion ...
beginning begin begin all over again every day do I want to be a saint
or a famous writer? Crazy I got went.

> (The trio concludes. Jack alone on the mountaintop. Lights
> down. End of scene.)

Scene Seven.

Desolation Peak. The High Cascades. Summer, 1956.

(Lights up on Jack who is sitting in the posture of Buddhist meditation on the mountaintop, a high platform upstage centre. There is
only the slightest suggestion it is a mountain. The scene is thirty days
in the wink of an eye. Open with a long pause.)

JACK: Sorry is the one
        who shoulders the world
        on bended back;
        Happy is the one
        who carries the face of God
        in an empty sack
        — so saith Kerouac.
        (Pause)

I'll always remember these lazy afternoons of Buddha-drifting sun and
cloud over Desolation Mountain. (Short pause) All I have to do, all
day long, is fetch a bucket of snow from the icefield, melt it down for
my drinking water, and then I can sit out here in the hot, sun-bright
grass and stretch like a cat. (Short pause) The ten directions sur-
rounded by sheer drops into silent gorges. (Yells) What is the meaning of the void?

        (Pause)

The first night I spent up here alone on the mountain, it was so quiet
the silence woke me in the middle of the night as if from a nightmare.
What is it?

        (Pause)

Then, I see a star just above the dark shoulder of a gigantic black bear.
It's Mount Hozomeen from way over there in Canada. (Short pause)
I get up from my lonely bunk, the mice scattering beneath, and I go
outside to black mountain shapes all around the black sky. Jack
Mountain. Three Fools Peak. Freezeout Peak. Golden Horn. Mount
Terror. Mount Fury. Mount Despair. Crooked Thumb. Baker. Chal-
lenger. And finally my own ... Desolation.

        (Pause. Jack sings like Sinatraa full verse from a 50s pop/jazz

46

tune. Pause.)

Wait, breathe, eat, sleep, cook, chop, fetch, write, watch ... wait. (Short pause) Thirty days go by, counting. (Yells) What is the meaning of the void?

(Pause)

Well well ... well look who's here. Ti Pousse. Little Nut. Little Fatty. Come on, come and get it. (Short pause) Good afternoon to you, Mr Mouse. How's the Missus? Come on, come on. Plenty of crumbs for everyone. (Short pause) Gerard? Can you see me now? I'm Jack Saint Francis Kerouac feeding all of God's humble creatures. Here you go. Hah, what's famous compared to this? New York, Beat Generation, bullshit. (Short pause) Gerard ... I know you can see me from up there in Heaven. All your little buddies are here. You can see me, can't you? I know you can. Come on fella, come on ... yeah.

(Pause)

Wait, breathe, eat, sleep —

(Sudden thunder and lightning.)

Sourdough, Sourdough ... Desolation Lookout calling Sourdough ... come in, Sourdough ... over.

(Thunder and lightning.)

A strike of lightning has just hit Skagit Peak ... There's a huge orange spot, like a geyser, a hell of a fire ... over.

(Pause)

Fifteen miles to the south, just east of Ruby Peak ...

(Thunder and lightning.)

Oh, my god, there's another one right beside it ... orange verticals of fire, but, but they seem to come and go, one minute they're there, then suddenly nothing. What's happening?

(Thunder and lightening.)

There's another, And another. And another. The whole world is on fire. The whole world is on fire.

(Pause. Sudden silence. Jack hears a snap like a twig breaking.)

What's that? Sasquatch.

(Jack helter skelters.)

Come here, you little shit, come here, you little shit, come here, you little shit, come here, come here.

(Jack kills a mouse.)

47

Oh Buddha Jesus God ... Oh Buddha Jesus God ... deliver us from the fires of consciousness beyond the void ...

(Pause)

Saint Gerard. Gerard. Are you there? Are you?

(Pause)

I, I ... I killed a ... I killed a mouse. (Short pause) Gerard ... How can you ever forgive me? ... Gerard ... sweet sweet Saint Gerard.

(Lights begin to fade. End of scene.)

Scene Eight.

North Carolina. Summer, 1956. Three time zones away.

(Lights up on Gabrielle as she lights a devotional candle in the tenement apartment.)

GABRIELLE: Saint Gerard, I resort to thy protection and aid and as proof of my affection and faith I offer this light which I shall burn every night.

> (The lights shift to the jazz club. Jack is at the mike.)

JACK: Begin begin begin beyond oh never again a pure vision ... begin beyond the crystal light point of the diamond sutra pine branch miles above the boiling cities ... begin beyond the visions of the mountain Desolation falling all the way down to the sea the tiny mouse scream a thorn of pain between my ears rubble avalanche crucifixion.

> (The lights shift to the apartment. Gabrielle lights a devotional candle.)

GABRIELLE: Saint Gerard, comfort me in difficulties and through the great favor which you enjoy by lodging in the house of Our Saviour, intercede for our family that we may always hold God in our hearts and be provided for in our necessities. I beseech thee to have infinite pity in regard to the favor I ask thee.

> (The lights shift to the jazz club.)

JACK: Begin beyond I begin to wander frantic crack-up low moaning sorry for myself to and fro fellaheen Ishmael ... begin beyond the wild west Arizona desert I cry for a vision the world upside down shaking me like ragdoll losing I.D. and my mind ... begin beyond Mexico City I sleep like garbage in an alley my companions a sick yellow dog and a stunted tree of withered leaves rosary Madonna catalogue of needle tracks benzedrine dreams ... begin beyond Tangiers I hear the deep bark of the ocean floor where a dark flute smothers a small child in a white cave ... begin beyond Paris I learn nothing the hard way c'est la vie pissoir satori ... begin beyond London I mix gin and sad loveless gloom underground with the blind worms at Stonehenge.

(The lights shift to the apartment. Gabrielle lights a devotional candle.)

GABRIELLE: If you please, my Lord, bless my poor Jackie and bring him back to me so we can live our little life together in peace, without pain. We have suffered so much, enough for two dozen families, and I haven't said a word. (Short pause) Saint Gerard, have pity on your poor wayward little brother, amen.

(The lights shift to the jazz club.)

JACK: Begin beyond Times Square Manhattan Island I talk to New York I talk to the godless ... I begin to lie and to be lied to ... I begin to drink drink and to be drunk grunt grunt like pig at trough drunk drink ... I begin to puke and to fuck and to be fucked swallowing opium raw nightmare enlightenment and final collapse.

(The lights shift to the apartment. Gabrielle lights a devotional candle.)

GABRIELLE: I ask thee, Saint Gerard, to cover the earth at Jackie's feet with a shower of roses as the Madonna did shower the schoolyard in your vision of Heaven on Earth.

(Pause)

Our Father. Hail Mary. Glory be.

(The lights shift to the jazz club.)

JACK: "All creatures tremble from fear of punishment," said Buddha ... begin beyond I got to do something different, wake up and smell the blood drying on my split lip wake up and slow down and try to stay alive ...

(The lights begin to fade on the jazz club. End of scene.)

Scene nine.

A small apartment. Berkeley, California. Summer, 1957.

(A spot follows Jack into the apartment.)

JACK: Begin beyond the next year the summer of 1957 in San Francisco in California and I'm living with my mother ... every time I see her she keeps growing older ... a little apartment at 1943 Berkeley Way ... sitting on the toilet in the bathroom through the window you can see the Golden Gate Bridge ... the golden gate to the Orient and the Buddha's perfect denial of perfectionless charm ... and I'm living with my mother enough with division and death I will tune my body to the hot California sun wean my mind on cheap tokay wine and I will rise newborn like a spring tree abloom growing straight up out of the rubble of a busted sidewalk ... begin beyond the beginning of famous twelve-thousand eight-hundred seventy-five days away from my birth ... Oh, and I'm living with my mother begin begin begin.
>   (Lights up on the apartment. Gabrielle and Jack are watching T.V., one of the classic 50s sitcoms. Each has a glass of wine, and a mostly-full gallon jug of red wine is nearby. Jack wears a bathrobe and is barefoot. For a moment, the lights illuminate a rather grotesque and pathetic Madonna and child.)

Mama ... why do you let men hurt you like that and just shrug it off?
>   (Pause)

Pourquoi?

GABRIELLE: Que c'est qu'tu dis-là?

JACK: The violence last night.

GABRIELLE: Quelle violence?

JACK: The man in the bar last night who you were flirting with.

GABRIELLE: Ch'flirtais pas.

JACK: What do you call it?

GABRIELLE: He was chasing my ass.

JACK: When you came back into the bar from outside ... what did you do, go out to his car or something?

GABRIELLE: I step outside to smoke a cigarette. T'es pas mon pere, toé?

JACK: There was blood in your mouth.

GABRIELLE: No, y'avait rien.

JACK: Look at your lip in the mirror, it's all swole up.

GABRIELLE: I bump into a door.

(Pause)
JACK: I love you, Mama. I love you like the Buddha loves the cessation of being.

(Pause)
GABRIELLE: Don't spill it.

JACK: Lots more where that came from.

GABRIELLE: When we get down to the last drink, it's mine because you spilled yours.

JACK: Here we got all the tokay wine in the whole state of California, and you're bitching about it.

GABRIELLE: The last drink's mine.

JACK: You'll be snoring like a long lonesome lonely freight train long before this bottle hits bottom.

GABRIELLE: The last drink's mine.

JACK: Okay. Don't pinch. (Short pause) Top you up right now.

GABRIELLE: I bought it in the first place.

JACK: Let's not forget that.

GABRIELLE: I'd like to know who else.

JACK: Yeah, yeah.

GABRIELLE: You?

JACK: Watch the television, okay?

GABRIELLE: Watching television til it's coming out my ear. Television, television ... all you ever do.

JACK: All you ever do.

GABRIELLE: How many hot bath did you take today?

JACK: I wasn't counting.

GABRIELLE: What's this hot bath and television? For that, you dragged me all the way from Florida?

JACK: I didn't drag you.

GABRIELLE: Three day and night on a stinking bus.

JACK: I looked after you the whole time.

GABRIELLE: You have to sleep sitting up. You have to eat out of a paper sack. Drunk puking in the aisle, brat squalling, old men snoring, sailor fighting, teenager masturbating ... I saw them, under their mag-

53

azine. And the worst part was every three or four hundred miles, a new driver with a smile as big as Niagara Falls would get on and announce, "Have a pleasant ride." Baise mon cul, pleasant ride.

JACK: But we always had a bottle.

GABRIELLE: And who got the lion share of that?

JACK: You had your cola and aspirin three times a day to soothe your nerves.

GABRIELLE: A poor old woman living out of a suitcase on a stinking bus for three day and night and you begrudge her an extra aspirin.

JACK: That's all you were allowed. It said so on the bottle.

GABRIELLE: Stingy puss tightwad.

JACK: I was looking after you, Ma.

GABRIELLE: I was looking after myself.

JACK: I bought you that pillow. I made sandwiches. I took you places. Remember New Orleans? We had a lot of fun there.

GABRIELLE: I remember sweating like a hog on a spit.

JACK: You met that nice old guy.

GABRIELLE: Who was that?

JACK: The bartender on Bourbon Street.

GABRIELLE: Him?

JACK: You got along really well, you talking about Papa, and he was talking about his dead wife.

GABRIELLE: Fat chance I'll ever hear from the like of him.

JACK: You might.

GABRIELLE: No.

(Pause)

JACK: You liked Mexico. We spent a whole afternoon walking around the streets of Juarez.

GABRIELLE: I liked the little church.

JACK: Iglesia de Santa Maria de Guadalupe.

GABRIELLE: I wanted to go into that church and light a candle for your papa.

JACK: The only person we could find inside was a barefoot Indian woman in a black shawl. She was crawling on her knees across the stone floor toward the altar.

GABRIELLE: She carried a little baby wrapped in rags.

JACK: She was praying.

GABRIELLE: A penitenté.

JACK: She was a sinner and didn't want God to forget her.

GABRIELLE: What was happening there? That poor little woman couldn't sin against God. Was her husband in prison? And that little baby wrapped up tight in a little ball, not a peep. Why?

JACK: I don't know why.

GABRIELLE: The Indian in Mexico believe in God just like us. And they pray to Marie. I never saw anything like that before.

JACK: And then we went for a walk to the park through the mud and chickens the smell of the market. Remember the little man with the bird in the cage who could tell your fortune?

GABRIELLE: Yes. I gave him a peso.

JACK: And the bird rummaged around in a pile of folded pieces of paper in the bottom of the cage and picked one up with its beak.

GABRIELLE: My fortune.

JACK: "You will have good fortuna with one who is your son who love you say the bird."

GABRIELLE: Stupid bird.

JACK: No, it wasn't.

GABRIELLE: Then where's my fortune? Huh?

JACK: It wasn't a stupid bird.

GABRIELLE: Where's my furniture? Where's my cat?

JACK: Tyke's okay.

GABRIELLE: How do you know?

JACK: You want to call him up, talk to your cat on the phone? Do it.

GABRIELLE: Sticking me here in California, a poor lonely old woman. That's my fortune.

JACK: I spend all my time with you, Mama.

GABRIELLE: Sure you do.

JACK: I do.

GABRIELLE: Yeah ... sneaking out of the apartment every night after you think I'm asleep ... running around with your friend Neal Cassidy and those other bums.

JACK: One night. I went to a poetry reading.

GABRIELLE: Poetry. Your brother Gerard was a saint, and what are you, what are you?

JACK: I'm a writer.

GABRIELLE: You're a bum is what, a bum.

JACK: That's not true because I work ... work all the time.

GABRIELLE: You couldn't support yourself on crutches.

(Pause)
JACK: I wish I'd never been born.

GABRIELLE: Thirty years ago, you shoulda died instead of Gerard.
(Pause)
Did you hear me? (Short pause) Did you?

JACK: I did die.

GABRIELLE: When did you die?

JACK: Last summer on the mountaintop when Gerard came down from Heaven.

GABRIELLE: Where is he then?

JACK: He's a rainbow over Desolation.

GABRIELLE: Sure he is.
     (The doorbell rings.)
Where do you think you're going?

JACK: To get the door.

GABRIELLE: I'm talkin to you.
     (Doorbell rings again. Jack is at the door.)
Calvaire, I hate California, I hate the fog, I hate the earthquake, I hate
the bum. At least in Florida, I had my cat.

     (Jack returns with a parcel.)
JACK: Allright, allright.

GABRIELLE: What is it?

JACK: From New York. Maybe it's my book.
     (Jack opens the parcel.)
Wow. Look at this. Six advance copies of *On The Road*. Wow.

GABRIELLE: A dirty book by a bum.

JACK: I've waited so long ... so long. Whoopee. Touchdown. Come
on, let's dance.

GABRIELLE: Lache moi. I'm going to jig for a book?

JACK: You wanted it, too. It's a holy book.

GABRIELLE: What's holy?

JACK: A book of transcendence, Mama, for you, for me, the
redemption of the Kerouacs, our salvation, all that history, all that
flesh, Gerard, Papa, pain, poverty, the whole sour carnival of suffering
Hell is finally a broken wheel, Mama.

GABRIELLE: They send a check?

JACK: The checks are gonna come like rain from Heaven you'll need a wheelbarrow.

GABRIELLE: Sure I will.

JACK: My picture on the magazine covers, *Life, Time, Mademoiselle* ... T.V., *The Tonight Show, Jack Paar* ... Hollywood will make a movie, Brando's my star ... a year from now Frank Sinatra could be my best friend.

GABRIELLE: And where will I be?

JACK: Right by my side.
(The lights change. End of scene.)

Scene Ten.

Jazz club. A dream scene.

(Lights up on Jack helping Gabrielle to a seat at the table in the jazz club. Gabrielle looks around at the audience. There is a single red rose in a vase on the table. Jack gets up on the stool at the mike.)

JACK: "Visions of my Mother."
       (The trio begins to play a slow jazzy blues.)
Visions of my mother sitting lotus flower Buddha calm kitchen chair straightback redbrick sunset of all Brooklyn far far from Broadway frames the tender picture ... Visions of my mother wild electric calico cat fur spill melting at her feet ... Visions of my mother glued to football radio girl free gleeful shouting mantra prayer when I get the ball go Jackie go go ... Visions of my mother calling me home hamburg and boiled potatoes steam on the stove ... Visions of my mother hanging my laundry on line of sunshine string of white doves transcends my blear rags ... Visions of my mother pouring hot bacon grease over chicken gizzards to feed her little kitty ... Visions of my mother patting my head like a cat hey Ma it's me Jack ... Visions of my mother retelling the saintful tale of my brother Gerard a rosary of quiet tears the visionary voice of my mom ... Visions of my mother in a shower of red roses ... Visions of my mother tying little pot of nickels into worn toe of sock staineth with angel midnight woes ... Visions of my mother groaning in her sleep sad twisting sheets ghostly groanings of my dead father on the empty side of the bed ... Visions of my mother they don't make girls like my ma no more there's only one like her God broke the mold when he made my mother ... Visions of my mother oh Mama Mama you are my number one gal of visions oh yeah.
       (The trio concludes the number. Gabrielle applauds.)
I did it all for you, Mama.

       (Someone begins to bang loudly on the stagedoor.)
GABRIELLE: Sacrament, what is it?

NEAL: (offstage) Jack. Jack.

JACK: It's Neal.

NEAL: (Offstage) Open up. Jackkk ...
         (Neal enters.)
Ho, Jack, old buddy buddy buddy am I glad to see you have before you
now a genuine once in a lifetime ...

GABRIELLE: Get off the stage, Cassidy.

NEAL: Evening, Missus Kerouac.

GABRIELLE: Piss up a rope, Cassidy.

NEAL: That fifty bucks you owe me, Jack, I need it now fucking
horse in the fifth ...

GABRIELLE: What fifty bucks?

JACK: Shh ... Mama, let me handle this.

         (Gabrielle begins to exit.)
GABRIELLE: Your father Leo would know what to do. Leo would
take charge.
         (Gabrielle exits.)

JACK: I haven't got fifty bucks.

NEAL: There's a guy with a tireiron gonna bust my kneecaps if I
don't show up with fifty bucks.

JACK: I swear by the Buddha who never told a lie.

NEAL: You can do better than that this is Neal remember me New York
Denver San Francisco. I got you a job on the railroad. I shared my wife
with you. (Short pause) I loaned you fifty bucks.

JACK: Here.

(Jack reaches into his bathrobe.)
Take everything I got.
    (Jack throws a handful of pennys on the floor. Neal dives to
    pick them up.)

NEAL: Remember this, Jack, your best friend crawling on his hands
and knees.
    (Pause)
Sometimes I get so tired of living on the edge of my skin I get so tired
I am so very very tired, Jack ... the railroad the suburbs Carolyn the
kids car payments swimming pool piano lessons smoking too too
much pot and now my pony system whoosh ... there is something
monstrous green conspiratorial a giant seaworm swims inside the
ocean highway of my brain when it feeds it feeds on me.

    (Pause)
JACK: I used you. (Short pause) And Allen and Lucien and Carolyn
and Luanne. All my friends. I used you all in my book.

NEAL: No big deal. Pay your debts.

JACK: I changed things.

NEAL: (Laughs) You're telling me ... Jack Kerouac rewrote *On The
Road*. Oh, my god, on eight-and-a-half by eleven-inch paper.

JACK: Can you forgive me?

NEAL: Forgive yourself, Jack. Everybody does it, uses people, you're
not Buddha, you're not even Edgar Cayce. (Laughs) There's little tiny
mice some of us don't even have kneecaps, and then there's big fat
cats.

JACK: I killed a mouse on the mountaintop. I beat it to death with
my bare hands. I didn't mean to do it.

NEAL: Nobody does, Jack, but the little varmits just seem to get in the way of what you want to do.

JACK: Forgive me.

NEAL: Fifty bucks, I'll forgive you. Deal?

JACK: I told you I haven't got it.

NEAL: Then what the hell did you get for this famous?
          (Neal exits.)

JACK: Neal.
          (The lights change. End of scene.)

Scene Eleven.

Jazz club. New Years Eve, 1957.

(Jack is at the mike. He is dressed as at the top of the show. The trio plays a reprise of "Frisco to the Apple," and Jack picks it up where he left off much earlier. He gradually becomes more noticeably drunk in behavior and speech.)

JACK: Sioux City, Iowa ... (Short pause) Correctionville ... Des Moines ... Colfax ... Marengo ... West Liberty ... Rock Island, Illinois ... Cicero ... Chicago ... Lafayette, Indiana ... Kokomo ... Tipton ... Fairmount ... Delphos, Ohio ... Upper Sandusky ... East Liverpool ... Chester, Pennsylvania ... Pittsburgh ... Altoona ... Pottsville ... Bethlehem ... America, when that blue centerlight goes pop in the middle of one of those fabulous yellow roman candles and the night spreads into a spider of light ... America, your children explode ... your children, the Buddhas of innocence incarnate, what's happening? ... wow ... Phillipsburg, New Jersey ... Plainfield ... Newark ... Hoboken... wow ... New York City, New Yawkkkk whoa —

   (Jack collapses. The trio stops playing and exits as the lights go down. End of scene.)

Scene Twelve.

Jazz club. New Years Eve, 1957. After hours.

(Stage lights up on Jack alone. He is drinking and singing. Everybody else has gone home or elsewhere to party.)

JACK: "He was just a wayward angel falling through the sky ... He was just a wayward angel falling ..."

          (A GUY in a grey flannel suit enters.)
GUY: Hey, Beatnik King.

JACK: "Oh, Lord, have mercy on his soul."

GUY: Hey, beatnik. I'm talking to you.

JACK: No, no you're a victim victim of Madison Avenue bullshit image machine, daddy-o.

GUY: Don't call me daddy-o, beatnik.

JACK: The word the word is beat like beaten down the brown fella-heen of the equatorial earth like beatitude.

GUY: Stay away from my wife.

JACK: Where where's your wife?

GUY: Stay away from her.
          (He hits Jack.)

JACK: Hey hey, man, I didn't touch anybody's wife.

GUY: Don't breathe on her.
          (He hits Jack.)

JACK: I'm going to sit down now and pray for you.

GUY: Get up and fight like a man.
          (He hits Jack.)

JACK: I'm a mouse not a man.

GUY: Get up and fight, Beatnik King.
          (He kicks Jack.)

JACK: Saint Gerard loves you.
          (Lights come down. End of scene.)

Scene Thirteen.

The theatre. The present.

(Gabrielle sits in the armchair lit by the glow of the T.V. In her arms and lap, she cradles a dead tabby cat. She is moaning.)

GABRIELLE: Teak ... Teak ...Teak ... Teak ... Teak ... Teak ... Teak ...Teak ... Teak ...

(Gabrielle drifts as if asleep. Jack enters.)
JACK: I walk across the stage to pull the curtain to my story, to shatter realities like atoms and stack them one atop the other like clouds yawning in eternity. And you follow, wherever it coheres and jellos, because you want to be told a story of how it went with Jack becoming a saint becoming Buddha becoming the void becoming me tonight ... but it's all illusion, vanity, wake up.
(Jack claps his hands. Gabrielle starts, sits up awake. Jack is climbing the mountain.)
Gerard est mort!

(Gabrielle can hear Jack but can't see him.)
GABRIELLE: Jackie?

JACK: It's alright, Mama.

GABRIELLE: Jackie? Where are you?

(Jack is on the mountain.)
JACK: Up in Heaven. I'm a saint now.

GABRIELLE: A saint to make the dog cry. Good luck.

JACK: Jack Kerouac died for your sins.

GABRIELLE: Sure you did.

JACK: We all die.

GABRIELLE: 'Good, damn it, good.

JACK: We grow by suffering.

GABRIELLE: Jesus God, by now I ought to be as big as a house.

JACK: Heaven is earth, and earth is Heaven, but we don't know it yet, forever and ever more, amen.

    (Pause)
GABRIELLE: Light a candle for your brother, Jackie.

    (Jack lights a candle.)
JACK: Begin begin begin ...

GABRIELLE: Les mauva. Les mauva.
    (The candle is the only light. End of scene.)

Scene Fourteen.

Orlando, Florida. A Vision.

(Lights come up on the trio playing a version of George and Ira Gershwin's "Someone To Watch Over Me." Jack is on the mountain. Gabrielle sees him now. Fabulous yellow roman candles. A shower of red roses.)

GABRIELLE: Jackie.

JACK: I love you, Mama.

GABRIELLE: Moi-aussi, Ti-Jean.
        (The trio continues to play as the lights go slowly down. End of scene.)

END OF PLAY

Straight Ahead

Straight Ahead was first produced by the New Play Centre at the Waterfront Theatre, Vancouver, in April, 1981, with the following cast:

LOUISA POTTER   Nicola Cavendish

Directed by Kathleen Weiss.

Straight Ahead was subsequently produced with *Blind Dancers* by Toronto Free Theatre as part of the Toronto Theatre Festival in May, 1981, with the following cast:

LOUISA POTTER   Rosemary Dunsmore

Directed by Henry Tarvainen.

Player:

LOUISA POTTER, aged 24.

Time:

Early evening, August, 1945.

Place:

The edge of a woods bordering a threshing field.

A section of rail fence stage left. A large tree that somewhat resembles "The Tree of Life" in the veins of a placenta stage right. Centrestage is wide and bare.

Big Band music, probably Glenn Miller, is playing. Something upbeat and patriotic. Lights. Music cuts back. A truck engine grinds up close offstage and shuts off. Pause. LOUISA comes onstage with a picnic basket full of goodies. She dances as she walks. She goes toward centrestage, stops and waves at the fence.

Louisa speaks all parts in the script.

LOUISA: Hey, you guys. Dad. Come and get it.
            (Pause. Louisa makes up a picnic. She bebops as she works.)
That oughta do it.
            (She picks up a red flag from the basket, goes to the fence and
            climbs it. She waves the flag.)
Dad! Hey, fellas! Howdy! Hey, yip! Will one of you look here? (Looks hard into the field) That guy looks just like Roy. (Short pause) Is that Roy on the wagon or who the hell is it anyway? (Hollers) Hey, you jay birds, come and get it!
            (Pause. She turns and sulks.)
They don't even pretend to see me. Three men. (Gets an idea) My Dad. My Boyfriend. (Short pause) And my ex-husband ... Mike. (Quickly) And none of a one of them comes when I call. (Climbs on the fence, waves the flag) Roy! Hello! Oh, Roy, sweety. How-ow-dy! (Short pause) Ain't nobody out there got a hole in his stomach? (Turns away) Huh! (Climbs down) Too bad for em.
            (She goes to the picnic. Gives it the once over.)

(DAD'S VOICE) Mustard. Where's the mustard?
            (Digs into the basket.)

(LOUISA) Dad'll have conniptions he hasn't got his mustard. (Finds the mustard) Let's see here. Mustard, ketchup, hot chillies, horse radish ... yuck! Maybe the old fart will choke on it. (Looks at the fence) Ain't they comin? Dad says to have a spread of food out here by six o'clock

74

this evening, so's I run my butt off all day long, and what's he do?

(DAD'S VOICE) And don't forget lots of mustard if you're going to make a potato salad.

(LOUISA) Huh. That man wouldn't eat nothing without the kick of a mule on his spoon. (Short pause) If I wasn't here like I was told, Dad would be yelling, "Where's that girl?" Well, here I am.
    (She goes back to the fence.)
How-dy! Wup wup, wuppy! Roy, look at me dammit. You don't have any trouble finding me in the orchard when the lightning bugs are dancing. Hello! Wup, wup! (Short pause) Mike!
    (Pause. She gets down. Feels nausea. Drops the flag.)
I thought it was called morning sickness. (Short pause) Baby, you bring the roll of the ocean in the night. But, please, don't roll me so low when Dad's setting down to his supper, or he'll light into me like a match touching gasoline. I know you're a part of me, a baby in me. Settle now, and Dad'll just eat and drink and chew at his tobacco. Settle now, and let him worry about the wheat on the south hill, not the seed inside his daughter. Let him get worked up about the thresher breaking down, not a bastard. (Short pause) And Mike. We can't let him suspect nothin' either. We can't let him know about you and me at all. (Jerks forward) No. Please, they may be comin'. Oh, baby, settle, and Mama will sing you a little song. How's that? Mama sing a song. (Moves away from the fence) Wish I had a cigarette.
    (Pause. She sings.)

> I can get it for you wholesale.
> I can get it for you
> First thing in the morning.
> I can get it for you
> Quick as it comes.

> I can get it for you
> Every day ... passing away.
> I can get you a rainbow.

75

I can get a bow and a ribbon store
For you.

I can get it for you wholesale.
I can get it for you
First thing in the morning.
I can get you a rainbow
Every day ... passing away.

(Short pause) Pretty good, huh? Maybe that song'll get me on "Lucky Strike" someday. Atlantic City. The Tommy Dorsey Orchestra. And featuring the sweet success loved by Americans everywhere ... la de dah ... Louisa Potter. Potter? Bought her. Got her. Potter will never do. Have to change my name to be a star. How about Poyle? Louisa Poyle. No, too stuck up. Maybe ... Pool. Yeah, I'll be Lou Pool, America's sweet success.

(A MALE RADIO ANNOUNCER'S VOICE) Ladies and gentlemen, Lou Pool.

(LOU POOL'S VOICE) Howdy, folks.

(ANNOUNCER'S VOICE) Well, Lou, this broadcast is going into ten million American homes tonight. Pretty big step for a country girl. Are you nervous?

(LOU POOL'S VOICE) Only when I take a breath.

(ANNOUNCER'S VOICE) I'm sure the boys in the band are waiting for that.
        (Boys in the band murmuring.)

(LOU POOL'S VOICE) That's why I'm holding my breath.
        (Canned laughter.)

(ANNOUNCER'S VOICE, laughing along) That's because you're nervous.
(LOU POOL'S VOICE) No ... so I don't lose my dress.
        (Canned laughter.)

(ANNOUNCER'S VOICE) Well, Lou, you sure do look good tonight.

(LOU POOL'S VOICE) Yeah, a real bombshell. They'll love me in Nagasaki.
    (They are cut off the air. Pause.)
Kapow! (Delivering a punchline) So he slaps me across the face with a wet towel. (Short pause) That's my Dad! He was just your regulation tight-fisted, narrow-minded, God-fearing, God-defying, hard-drinking, hard-working, hard-hearted son of a gun. And he was mean. You know the joke about Christmas? Somebody says, "What did you find in your socks?" And the answer is, "My father's feet!" I was lucky to find an i.o.u. for a good beating behind the barn. I was lucky to find my socks. My dad was so mean, his shadow walked on tippy-toes, his footprints ran away ... the other way. Hi-ho, Silver! (Short pause) He was so mean ... say "good morning" to him, and you were asking for trouble. (Short pause) He was so mean he threw the money for my high school ring in my face.

    (Out of Lou Pool character, she screams.)
(LOUISA) You son of a bitch.
    (Jerks her head as if she's been hit in the face. Drops to the floor. Crawls around.)

(DAD'S VOICE) You made me, girl. You made me, girl.

(LOUISA) I can't see.

(DAD'S VOICE) You can see. You can see.

(LOUISA) I can't see.

(DAD'S VOICE) Open your eyes. Louisa, open your eyes.

(LOUISA) I can't, I can't.

(DAD'S VOICE) Louisa.

(LOUISA) I can't see!

(Pause. She regains a little composure.)
I couldn't see for crying out loud. I couldn't ... see. (Short pause) I felt like Jonah in the belly of the whale. Blind Jonah. (Short pause) Oh, baby. Nine month long you'll be a blind fish in my belly.

(Gets to her feet. Slaps her hands together.)
Kapow! (Goes to the fence) What if they come, and they hear me? What if they do? They'll think I'm dumb. That's all I hear. Dumb girl. Dumb broad. Dumb bell. Dumb chick. Dumb bitch. Dumb cunt. Dumb slit. Dumb twit. Dumb hole. Dumb ass. Dumb fuck. Dumb, dumb, dumb. (Short pause) Dumb house. (Short pause) Dumb sky. (Short pause) Dumb cloud. (Short pause) Dumb sun. Dumb moon. Dumb earth. Dumb world. (Whispers) Kapow. (Short pause) Dumb Nagasaki. (Kicks the picnic) To hell with their supper. (Short pause) I better clean it up. (Ignores it) 'Cept maybe Mike. He's the only one. (Goes to the fence) Mike! Wup! Wup! Hello! Mike! (Recognition at last) Whoa, Mike! Wah, hoo hoo hoo! Yeah, come and get it, you three-legged devils, there's enough mustard in the potato salad to kill the bunch of you. (Laughing) Oh, that Mike, he's my kind of man, eating out of my hand. He's sure no be-bopper, but I love my husband. Ex-husband. I left Mike to go running with Roy. Ha. Then I dumped on Roy to get into radio. And before you could say "straight ahead" there I was, Lou Pool, America's Sweet Success, starring in my first movie role, the true story of yours truly. (Short pause) Three o'clock in the morning under the light of a half moon. A garden swing where the fence is now, and a white clapboard farmhouse has replaced the tree. The house is dark, and a dozen crickets chirp along with the popcorn munchers at the picture show. Mike, my good Mike, is sleeping and tossing and turning on the swing. Oh, a close-up of his face. It's Alan Ladd all mixed up with Victor Mature. He's so darned good-looking, dressed in a new suit, dark blue, but it's all rumpled up and dusty, and his tie is loose and mussed-up. The poor boy's having a time staying on the swing, and his face is sad and very tired. (Short pause) Then, there's the sound of a car coming to a screaming stop in front of the house. Mike's in the backyard, but it wakes him up. A car door opens, and the air is filled with drunken chatter and laughter and a car radio playing a big band number. The door slams shut, and the car backs up and drives away. (Short pause) Mike!

(MIKE'S VOICE) I'm real. I'm real.

(LOUISA) Mike, you're going to break my arms.

(MIKE'S VOICE) I had to sneak through the window of my own house. What'd you do? Spend the money and burn the letters?

(LOUISA) You come here and been waiting so you could make love to me. I like to be made love to very much.

(MIKE'S VOICE) You broke everything you touched.

(LOUISA) I didn't want it like that.

(MIKE'S VOICE) And the night you left me ... the night the daisy chain sort of fell apart and the rains come down and ground the petals into the mud and the sun come up and baked the mud dry and the wind blew the dust across the fields ... you didn't want it like that?
         (Louisa is shaken. Pause. She leans back on the fence as if she
         is Lou Pool ready to sing a number in a nightclub. She sings,
         in Lou Pool's voice.)

                    Going to get me a man
                    And pour him like a whisky in a glass.
                    Going to get me a man —
                    Hallelujah, to ball my ass.

                    Don't care if he's black or Jew
                    Don't care if he's fat or slow,
                    Or if he's weird — wants a blow —
                    I don't care ...
                    Then he lets me go
                    My own way.

                    Pretty awful rhymes,
                    These ugly times
                    ... Nagasaki ...

79

Just so he lets me go
My own way.

(Speaks) Don't so much want a husband ...
What's a husband?
Sounds like a bee in need
Of a bandaid — right?
Sounds like a dude
Wanting a steady paycheck,
Thirty year mortgage,
And me tying up tomato plants
In back of the garden patch.
What do I think of that?

(Sings) Why don't he let me go
My own way?

Going to get me a man
And pour him like a whisky in a glass.
Going to get me a man —
Hallelujah, to ball my ass.

(Speaks) Instead I get these guys who
Doesn't like a woman to smoke a cigarette.
I like a cigarette,
Especially after a meal.
Who the hell are you, honey?
I likes to smoke.
That gets their dander up ...
Or something up.
(Sings) Oh, give me a man who lets me go
My own way.

(She takes a bow. Applause. She starts to leave the stage, her
nightclub act complete, but stops short.)
Today, we dropped an atomic bomb on Nagasaki, Japan, and it was ...
(Breaks off, takes a breath.)

(LOUISA) I spent the afternoon over a hot stove fixing a meal for a bunch of men who ain't showed up. Fried chicken. I'll name my baby "Little Nagasaki."

(Pause. She moves swiftly away.)

Thank Christ, they finally see'd me though. (Goes to the fence) What they doin' now? Fooling with a shuttle cock or some thingamajig? Men. Who needs 'em?

(Walks away. Pause. She is sick again.)

I never seen the ocean, but I swear there's a sea sickness in me. Feel like a boat a drifting and drifting into the fist of a storm. Oh, baby, maybe it'll smash up, bump us into an island somewheres. I can't stand the taste of fish in my mouth.

(Pause)

We was out on Cotter's Hill. Roy picked up some fish and fries to go ... I hate fish ... and we drove up there ... ahem ... to listen to the corn grow. You'd be surprised what country folk have to do to have a good time. (Short pause) Well ... Roy pulled up some fish hooks out of his pants pocket, and I was just astonished. Big black ants swarming over a shattered jar. I wanted to cry.

(She cries.)

(ANNOUNCER'S VOICE) Tell the folks out there a little about yourself, Lou.

(LOU POOL'S VOICE) I'm five feet two, eyes of blue ... or at least that's what it says on this card.

(Canned laughter.)

(ANNOUNCER'S VOICE) You don't look a foot over six feet.

(Canned laughter.)

(LOU POOL'S VOICE) I'm left-handed.

(ANNOUNCER'S VOICE) That's handy.

(LOU POOL'S VOICE) Watch it, buster, I lead with my right.

(Canned laughter.)

(ANNOUNCER'S VOICE) Maybe we better have another song.

(LOU POOL'S VOICE) Okay. How about "Give Me A Light From Your Cigarette"?

(ANNOUNCER'S VOICE) You can't smoke while we're on the air.

(LOU POOL'S VOICE) That's the name of the song.
    (Canned laughter. Pause. She sings in Lou Pool's voice.)

>   Give me a light from your cigarette
>   And I'll try to forget.
>   Each minute I loved you
>   Is a week to forget.
>
>   Forget I ever met you,
>   Forget to forget.
>
>   Give me a light from your cigarette
>   And I'll smoke to the memories.
>   Each minute I loved you
>   Is a year of regret.
>   Forget the smiles on your face,
>   The creases in your pants.
>   Forget our favorite, private places,
>   All the nights that we danced.
>   Forget I ever met you,
>   Forget to forget.
>
>   Give me a light form your cigarette
>   And I'll try to forget.
>   Each minute I loved you
>   Is a lifetime's lament.
>
>   Forget I ever met you,
>   Forget to forget.

(Pause)

(THE VOICE OF A FAN ON THE STREET) Those big band ballads for a female lead really let a lady get it off her chest. My favorite? Lou Pool, who else? One of her ballads is worth a thousand ... there's just no comparison I can think of for sheer power of musical expression. Some girls can sing a song, but Lou Pool brings it to life. But I understand she's a very unhappy woman in her private life. I read in ... uh, somewhere that she gave up her kid to make it big on radio. And she never was married to the man.

(LOUISA) That's not true! It's a crock of bull! (Goes to the fence) What the hell you doin' now? One of em's on the ground. Are they drinking out there? Goddamn em. I should of stayed to the house and just got the warshing out. Or just sat on the porch swing and picked my toes. A man just wants to keep a woman astraddle the fence, and when he's got her there, then the hell with her. Don't matter who she is, oh no, just what she is to him ... a man's one-sided idea of a woman. Keeps her like a rat in a cage scrambling from one corner to another trying to sniff her way out. Only a woman is dumber than a rat because there's only one side to her cage ... a man's one-sided idea. All she got to do though is just walk away. Close up shop, walk away, just let it go. Straight ahead. (Short pause) I ain't a picnic in the woods.
    (Pause)
All right! Lights! Action! Camera! (Short pause) Okay, here's Roy, an average-sized dude, horny, warty as a frog and with a bit of a swagger. Wearing bib-overalls, he's filthy from head to foot with grain dust. His hands are cupped and filled with freshly-picked wild raspberries. The red juices run down his arms and folded cuffs. He munches at the berries, and juices run down his mouth so in black-and-white it looks like an open wound. He walks with his head down, so he don't see me, but I see him a comin.

(ROY'S VOICE) Jesus, don't we look like a couple of jay birds caught with our pants down.

(LOUISA) You didn't scare me. Get back, damn you, you stain my dress.

(ROY'S VOICE) You want a berry, Lou? A real ripe berry?

(LOUISA) I just want you to stay away from me.

(ROY'S VOICE) Now that's the nicest thing you said to me in days. It is a fact. What's eating you, Lou?

(LOUISA) Go to hell, Roy. Can't you see ... I'm recording.
      (She walks away. Pause. She sings in Lou Pool's voice.)

> Give me another heartache
> Now the last one's stopped.
> Had so many lately
> I think they're lollipops.
>
> Give me another heartache
> Just put it up on top.
> Had so many lately
> I think they're lollipops.
> I do.
> I think they're lollipops.

  (Applause.)

(LOU POOL'S VOICE) That's it.

(ANNOUNCER'S VOICE) You know, Lou, your name fits you well.

(LOU POOL'S VOICE) I thought it was a dress. Who wrote this line?
      (Canned laughter.)

(ANNOUNCER'S VOICE) I'm serious, Lou. Your eyes are deep pools of blue ... like the whole sky reflected in a pool of sparkling waters.

(LOU POOL'S VOICE) You're going to break for a brewery commercial?
      (Canned laughter.)

(ANNOUNCER'S VOICE) No, Lou, I'm serious about this. When I look into the pools of your eyes, I see America's sweet success. Motherhood and apple pie. Ladies and gentlemen ...

(Applause.)
I'm sure our listening audience agrees.

(LOU POOL'S VOICE) Thank you. Thank you. That's a very sweet thing for you to say. And when I look into your eyes, do you know what I see there?

(ANNOUNCER'S VOICE) No. What do you see?

(LOU POOL'S VOICE) Nagasaki.

(ANNOUNCER'S VOICE) Will you cut that out!
    (Blip — they are cut off the air.)

(LOUISA) Screw that. I don't want to be a star.
    (Pause)
Roy never did know his ass from a hole in the ground. But I was a fool and thought that he did. He was a railroader, and I was a dancer. It's the story of my life. When I found the rotten fish and maggots in a piece of newspaper under the car seat, I knew I had his seed in me. Knew it in a second. (Short pause) Knew I had a fish in my belly.
    (She goes to the fence.)
They are drinking out there. All three of em's down on the ground under the wagon. (Short pause) I'm going back to the house.
    (She walks away quickly, then slows down.)
But Mike doesn't drink ... (Short pause) Mike! But ...

(MIKE'S VOICE) You got to come and sit with me for a minute. I got to talk to you and look at you for just a minute. You got to come. You got to come.

(LOUISA) Okay, okay, let's go sit down a minute. It's okay, let's go and sit. (Short pause) Mike, it's okay. Everything is going to be okay.

(MIKE'S VOICE) It's not okay. Everything is shit.

(LOUISA'S VOICE) Everything is okay.

(MIKE'S VOICE) You've got to stop lying about it.
        (Louisa slips away from Mike.)

(LOUISA) You got any cigarettes, Roy? I left mine in a car somewheres.
I could use a smoke.

(ROY'S VOICE, slowly) Yeah, I think so.
        (Gives her a cigarette.)

(LOUISA) Thanks. You got a light?
        (Louisa goes back to where she left Mike.)
Mike ...

(MIKE'S VOICE) I saw you at the dance last night, Louisa. You're getting
to be a real high stepper on the dance floor.

(LOUISA) You was at the dance?

(MIKE'S VOICE) For a little while I was there.

(LOUISA) How come I didn't see you there?
        (Pause)
Mike! How come I didn't see you there?
        (Pause)
Mike?
        (Pause)
I got to have a little good times in my life. I earn my little bit of Saturday night fun. Everybody and his neighbor will say I shouldn't of kept
my baby. Somebody else should have him and not his mama. Why,
the day he was born a welfare man come walking into my hospital
room with papers to sign to give him away. I hadn't hardly had time
to wake up from my nap. A real hot dog salesman with a smile on his
face like Joe DiMaggio. This guy was hot all right, but I ain't nobody's
fool. The son of a bitch was after my baby. (Short pause) He was an
asshole. Just another man, just another asshole. "Social machinery,"
he says, the social machinery of the state capitol will feed and clothe
and raise my baby to be a nice young man. So I says to him, "Here's

86

your social machinery, Mr. Man. Here's what feeds my baby." And I pulled down my gown and shoved one of my tits into his nose. He looked like a kid blowing up a party balloon. Eyes popping like pop corn ... You ain't gettin my baby. You can't have him. (Short pause) I kept my baby. I kept my baby.

(MIKE'S VOICE) Stop lying.

(LOUISA) Mike ... please.

(MIKE'S VOICE) Just stop it. I'll see you later.

(LOUISA) Mike ...
        (She walks after Mike's voice. Then she goes to the fence.)
Something is wrong.
        (Pause)

(ROY'S VOICE) Too much mustard in the potato salad.

(LOUISA) Only way ... Roy, we got to have ourselves a talk.

(ROY'S VOICE)   What we been doin all along? (Grunts) We have more talks than Roosevelt and Churchill. But you got yourself another talk, spill it out.

(LOUISA) This is big, Roy.

(ROY'S VOICE)   Spill it out and get it over. I got to get back to the field to give the old man his breather.

(LOUISA) Dad can wait on his chicken and beer. (Short pause) I'm going to have a baby. (Pause) I said I'm going to ... honey, you're going to be a daddy.

(ROY'S VOICE)   What do you think this is? "The Lux Radio Theatre"? Maybe you got the woman's part, Lou, maybe you got one of them fat CBS contracts. I wouldn't know. But I ain't your star, Lou. I ain't your star.

(Louisa) I love you.

(Roy's voice) Love? (Short pause) You know what they're saying about you in the pool hall? Yulie Moss says if they turned you inside out they'd find more pricks in you than a porcupine. (Jerks back) Jesus, bitch, you cut my lip.

(Louisa) You'll live.
          (Louisa wanders about.)
If the shoe fits, wear it, huh? I've tried on so many shoes trying to please a man it don't matter anymore if I need a right shoe or a left. I put it on, and it fits fine all the same. I wear em all.
          (Pause)
I coupled all right, I slept with any man. (Short pause) I had to cheat on Mike. I had to run around.

(Mike's voice) You only cheated yourself.

(Louisa) I cheated on you, and you never got over it.

(Mike's voice) Tell the truth.

(Louisa) If I told the truth, would you stay here with me?

(Mike's voice) Tell the truth, you won't need me anymore.

(Louisa) I can't tell the truth.

(Mike's voice) I got to go. Here's my ride.

(Louisa) Mike. (Follows after him) No.
          (Pause)
Mike isn't out in that field tonight because Mike's dead. We got married, and six months later he joined the army. He was driving a truck. All I got back was dog-tags.
          (Pause)
I say that I cheat on my husband, I guess, because it sounds exciting

88

like people who get into all the magazines. (Short pause) Maybe it keeps him alive. Long as I'm cheating on Mike, he's walking around in the world.

(Pause)

Mike's dead. (Short pause) Roy ... he's just gone. Splitsville. I don't care. (Short pause) Those two guys with Dad, I don't know one of em from Adam.

(Pause)

So, I'm sorry, Mike, I'm sorry I lied and made you up tonight. I'm sorry I lied, but I don't think I can keep from lying tomorrow. (Short pause) Maybe it keeps me alive.

(Pause)

(Begins to giggle) I guess I'm about as alive as a body could ever be. Yes, I am. (Short pause) You and me, kid. We'll knock em dead.

(Sings)

> I can get you a rainbow
> Every day ... passing away.

(She hears something from the field. Goes to it.)

Dad! (Short pause) Are you drunk? (Laughs) Can you hear me? (Hollers) Dad! (Short pause) I'm gonna have a baby, and I'm gonna keep it. Maybe I'll walk barefoot through Hell, maybe I won't, but I'm gonna keep it, and if you don't like that, I hope you fall down on your butt and break something. (Cheerfully) Whoa, there, Grandpa, take care of yourself.

(Lights.)

END OF PLAY

Blind Dancers

Blind Dancers was first produced by the New Play Centre at City Stage, Vancouver, in February, 1979, with the following cast:

DELL MARTIN   Richard Newman

LOUISA POTTER   Beth Kaplan

Directed by Bob Baker.

Blind Dancers was subsequently produced with *Straight Ahead* by Toronto Free Theatre as part of the Toronto Theatre Festival in May, 1981, with the following cast:

DELL MARTIN   Michael Hogan

LOUISA POTTER   Rosemary Dunsmore

Directed by Henry Tarvainen.

Players:

DELL MARTIN, twenty-eight, a jazz trombone player.

LOUISA POTTER, twenty-six, a weekend bandchick.

Time:

Summer, 1947.

Place:

Toledo, Ohio.

A cheap but decent hotel room. The room has a window overlooking the street. Beside the bed is a bedside table, and on the table there are two glasses, a whisky bottle, an ashtray, and a Bible open to *The Song of Solomon*. Also in this room is a vanity with a mirror and a small stool. A woman's overnight bag, its contents strewn about. A small bowl-shaped sink. Towels. A couple of straightback chairs. One of them is near the foot of the bed, and a man's mussed and wrinkled black tuxedo has been haphazardly thrown against it. At the foot of the chair is an open trombone case. Though cluttered and lived-in, the room is large enough to turn about with freedom. Outside it is night, but there is enough light to clearly see two figures swing-dancing: LOUISA POTTER, a small-town girl come to the city for a weekend of shopping and dancing, and DELL MARTIN, a fourth-chair trombone player with an undistinguished big band. An assembled trombone lies on the bed. A pair of red panties is loosely tied to the curved end of the slide. The light from the window begins to brighten with Dell's monologue, and a person can read "Swing is King" soaped on the mirror of the vanity. The environment is bright, hot and muggy.

The movement of the characters is swift, precise and hovers in the orbit of dance. The voices are instruments, the bodies are dancers.

The language is a fantasy of pre-TV middle-American speech. A drawl isn't necessary, but each word does carry a certain amount of weight in time.

Lights begin to come up.

DELL: Say you blow a city, coming into the city, a pure, straight tone, a straight ahead zing, a kind of open blare that hits you right between the ears with a million squares of color. Coming into the city, you wouldn't see more than a sign or two in bright red or blue, spots of blue and red in a wide field of green and yellow like the colors of a harvest ... then it opens right up at the edge of the city ... up, up, more colors, more wild notes ... lots of red ... burr-rapp ... and a heavy blue ... mo-o-an ... more and more wild sounds of things inside the city. A bright, pure, busy sound of buildings and trees swaying, and sidewalks jumping and people hoofing it along. Bright trees, streets like brass in a bright city, and you need a bright instrument ... like trumpets that have a high, bright tone. And a shrill, noon-whistle blast, ships in port dragging their heavy chains, taxis honking ... honk, honk ... blaring in the melting intersections ... a city dazzling beside a glass sea with shoe clerks and secretaries, soda jerks and shop girls hustling, jiving, bopping down the sidewalks, the sunlight flashing like knife blades ... or cut crystal ... flashing off their bright scarves, their summer hats, their lunches balled-up in brown paper sacks.

LOUISA: (joining him in the jam) Now, you jazz me, you roll me with your bone now. Oh, Mr. Trombone Man, you got the slide and the horn to jazz me till I feel I just been born ... just opened my eyes and been born. You jazz me, you roll me with your straight-ahead bone.

DELL: (taking another breath) Then the colors suddenly shift, and the band blows a music that turns like a star falling out of the sky. Then it turns again, shifting fast and shifting hard, to a music that's dark and dull and dreary ... like midnight rain ... and you need lower sounds, bluesy, subtle sounds and colors that you only get out of a bass or a trombone ... then quick, quick ... coming at you like shots out of the dark ... then like ripples, ripples of brass and woodwind ... then waves. The open sea, and a green woods and hilltops of houses turning round a city of sound. Then a big wave that's bigger than all the other waves before it ... a wave huge and terrifying ... with a backwash of horrible, raw sound as if the whole bright city were suddenly thrown around in the waves, and the woodwinds are soaring like birds into oblivion.

LOUISA: (like singing the blues) Day come knocking, night come calling ... all my troubles rolled up in a ball. Well, I'll just roll them down to the corner store and buy myself a stick of peppermint candy. Candy's dandy, oh ... and liquor's quicker, but only the bone man, the slide trombone man's got the horn to oil me. Yeah, you jazz me ... jazz me with your trombone till I feel I just been born.

DELL: Bang! Coming down hard like a dam breaking, showering and swirling all the themes of color and sound ... an undertow of lowdown bass ... those fool birds again.

LOUISA & DELL: Yeah ... !

DELL: Like a shock, a sudden silence descends. The color is solid and
pure and calm ... the music of no sound.
> (Pause. Dell picks up the trombone and mimics playing the
> instrument. The red panties go up and down, waving like a
> flag on the end of the slide. Dell makes a few bops, a few blares
> on the horn as if he's warming up before really swinging out.)

Yeah. (Short pause) Ping! That's all folks.
> (Louisa undresses and slips under the covers into the bed.
> Dell undresses and joins her. Long pause. Dell emerges from
> the covers to get dressed in a pair of tuxedo pants and an
> undershirt. Slowly. Very slow and shaky. Dell is dumb-
> founded, bitter-sweetly half-awake and very hungover. Get-
> ting up from a hotel bed after dawn is a musician's infrequent
> luxury. He has missed his bus. He looks for his watch, goes
> through his pockets but is careful not to jangle any loose
> change or his metal key-ring. Louisa sits up in the bed and
> runs her hand down the length of the trombone's bell. She
> turns her head and looks at Dell. She is hungover as well but
> is content and fairly relaxed compared to Dell, whose move-
> ment is slow, calculated and fidgety.)

LOUISA: (brightly) Who's your all-time favorite trombone player?

DELL: (absently but kindly) Established guys?

LOUISA: Yeah, sure.

DELL: Hard to say. Jack Teagarden. Jack Jenney. They're classics.
(Short pause) Dorsey's okay. Kai Winding's got that fantastic bop.

LOUISA: What about Glenn Miller?

DELL: He's dead.

LOUISA: I know that.

DELL: Miller was a terrible trombone player. But a damn good band-leader. A bloodhound when it came to smelling money.
        (Dell gets down on all fours and crawls across the room.)

LOUISA: What's your favorite band, then?

DELL: That's a pretty big order, ain't it? Artie Shaw, Krupa, Kenton ... Jimmie Lunceford ... how many fingers and toes you got?

LOUISA: Ellington?

DELL: Superb.

LOUISA: I love that nigger music. How about the old-timers?

DELL: White guys? The Wolverines ... Ben Pollack. Black guys? They're all good.
        (Dell crawls around the floor and notices a couple of fat shop-ping bags. Absently, he puts his hand in one and pulls out a blue sleeper for a year-old baby. He looks at it incredulously.)

LOUISA: How about Paul Whiteman?
        (Dell looks at the sleeper, then he looks at Louisa. She refuses to acknowledge the sleeper in his hands.)
How about Paul Whiteman?

        (Dell puts the sleeper away.)
DELL: Paul Whiteman? That fat tub of shit?

LOUISA: Hah, you're okay, Trombone Man. I don't care for his stuff at all. He couldn't swing on a playground. But I swear my old man lis-tened to that fat tub of shit every Saturday night for fifteen years.

DELL: (getting to his feet) A lot of people did.
        (Dell finds his watch. He picks it up and winds it.)

97

Okay already. Ten minutes to six. We got that much anyways. (Short pause) Now, if we can only figure out what day it is.

LOUISA: (laughing) What day it is?

DELL: Uh-huh ... that's what I said.
        (Pause. Dell goes to the window and looks down at the street.
        Dell sees something on the street that he wishes wasn't there,
        but it is, and he stares out the window.)

LOUISA: You're screwy.

DELL: I think I been screwed all night.

LOUISA: It's Saturday morning, Bone Man. Can't you figure it out?
You blowed me out all night from the bandstand, then you blowed me
out till morning on this here bedstead.

DELL: People going to church, I suppose, on a Saturday morning?

        (Louisa starts to get up quickly from the bed and just as
        quickly sits back down again.)
LOUISA: (painfully) Oh.

        (Dell turns away from the window.)
DELL: So, you got it, too.

LOUISA: If your head's a beachball and your brains are razor blades,
I got it, too.

DELL: Don't fight it, whatever you do. Just try and take it easy, and
it'll be an easier day, guaranteed. Take it hard, and you got a day's
work in front of you.
        (Church bells ring up from the street. Dell and Louisa jump
        with fright.)
Shaky. Very shaky. (Short pause) Whew. Yeah, it's Sunday all right.
Hear them bells calling to the faithful.

98

LOUISA: How come we hear them so good?
(Louisa gets up from the bed, slips into her dress and goes to the window. Dell slaps his hands together with a smack.)
It can't be Sunday. I won't let it.

DELL: It is. It is. Damnit. (Short pause) I did it. I missed the bus. I missed a gig! (Shakes his head) I did it good.

LOUISA: Catholics go to church on Saturday.

DELL: In battalion strength? Look at the numbers down there. The beach at Iwo Jima didn't see that much action. (Short pause) I did it. Jack Daniels does it to me every time.

LOUISA: This is a joke. How far away's the bus station?

DELL: A couple of blocks, but you may as well relax. There ain't another bus out of this town for two hours. I know. I live in buses. (Short pause) Two blocks, two hours ... two jokes. You're looking at one, and I'm gawking at the other.

LOUISA: I ain't laughing.

DELL: Nobody said they was good jokes.
(Dell moves to the bedside table and picks up the bottle of whisky and two glasses.)

LOUISA: (to herself) I don't see no bus station.

DELL: Hair of the dog?

LOUISA: We sure must of let our hair down.

DELL: (catching the drift) Ha ... to a hair.

LOUISA: Let's not split hairs, Bone Man.

99

DELL: Well, I didn't mean to ... get into your hair.

LOUISA: You won't catch me ...

DELL: ... turning a hair? Ha.
>   (Dell pours two drinks at the bedside table. Glass clinks against glass, a little bit of whisky spills.)
Easy. Easy.
>   (Dell takes a glass to his lips and swallows the whisky in one gulp. He smacks his lips and coughs. He turns to Louisa and offers her the other glass of whisky.)
Here. This'll make your hair stand on end.

LOUISA: Or grow some on my chest.

DELL: They say strong drink makes strong men.

LOUISA: Who said that? A strong man or a drunk?
>   (Louisa takes a sip of whisky, swallowing it hard.)

DELL: Good old Jack. Kick of a mule, huh?

LOUISA: They'll have to pump my stomach to get the horseshoes out of my ass.
>   (Both of them start laughing. Louisa can't stop laughing. She goes to a chair and sits down with her drink.)

LOUISA: (after a moment, weakly) Sunday?

DELL: You becoming a believer?

LOUISA: No.

DELL: Well, you better, P.D.Q. We must of had a twenty-four hour blackout.

LOUISA: Sex and whisky at sixty miles an hour with the lights out.

(Dell's body shakes with the jitters.)

DELL: Yeah, something like that. (Short pause) Last time I drank two bottles of this stuff I destroyed the hotel room I was staying in. Smashed out all the windows with a chair, busting up all the furniture on the edge of the tub.

LOUISA: You're a rangatang.

DELL: It started out real innocent-like ... I was laughing and carrying-on with this redhead bandchick when I suddenly fell on my back into the bathtub. But that was all right, I was still laughing. But I got mad and blew my top when I couldn't pull myself out.

LOUISA: Afraid to get your feet wet?

DELL: Flat on my back, the tub twirling around like a little boy's top. Finally managed to get a hold on the shower curtain and pulled myself over the edge. (Short pause) That tub was my grave.

LOUISA: Now I heard it all. A casket with hot and cold running water.

DELL: Very uncasual like, I did a kamikaze on the room. The hotel is applying to the Marshall Plan for damages. The redhead screaming, chairs going off like shrapnel. Finally, I knocked over a half-bottle of Jack Daniels on the floor, and it stopped me cold. I thought for some reason it was my blood spilling across the rug instead of the whisky. I felt the rug soaking, sucking up my soul. And you know what? I jumped right into bed and passed out on the spot. (Short pause) The next morning the bandleader, Seab Wheeler, walks into my room to drag me down to the bus. Seab takes one look at the place, and all he can say is, "Martin, you've destroyed your room." (Short pause) I didn't remember a thing. The redhead told me what happened ... what she remembered anyway ... and I began to pick up the pieces like splinters of a broken chair.

LOUISA: This place is still pretty nice. We must be lucky the tub's down the hall.

DELL: Yeah. (Short pause) In fact, except for this bad head, I feel real peaceful, satisfied, like I haven't felt in a long, long time. Still, it must have been some kind of straight ahead, loop the loop blackout. (Short pause) What do you remember, honey?

LOUISA: Hmm ... I remember being horny and wanting to get balled by a guy real bad. I like big bands, I like to swing, so I went to your dance last night.

DELL: Correction. Two nights ago.

LOUISA: We ain't sure of that.

DELL: I'm sure ... and ... sure as old swing is king, it must be getting home to you, too.

LOUISA: Okay, you're so smart, what happened to Saturday?

DELL: I wish I knew ... I wish I knew.
        (Dell notices a piece of parchment paper on the vanity and
        picks it up.)
Holy cow. This takes the cake.

LOUISA: What?

DELL: Oh, no. Ha. Oh, yes. Oh, boy. This. This takes the cake on a loop the loop.
        (Holding the parchment, Dell sweeps his hand away from his
        body and half bows to Louisa.)
You're Louisa ... Louisa Potter, I presume?

LOUISA: Yeah ... so?

DELL: Well ... we better get to know each other a little bit. Uh, "Twenty Questions"?

LOUISA: Look, Bone Man, I slept with you because I had a one night

102

hankering for a man. This ain't a tryout for a radio quiz show.

DELL: Oh yeah? Looks as if we've already hit the jackpot.

LOUISA: You're a screwball.

DELL: Okay, okay. We're going to ... get married.

LOUISA: The day Bing Crosby craps on Christmas.

DELL: Look ... here's the license.

LOUISA: Let's see that thing.
(Dell hands the parchment to Louisa.)

DELL: Just like that Clark Gable movie ...

LOUISA: You Dell Martin?

DELL: At your service, my lady.

LOUISA: I ain't your lady.

DELL: I ain't Clark Gable.

LOUISA: Umph.

DELL: Sorry.

LOUISA: This ain't no license.

DELL: It ain't? I suppose it's a trolley transfer?

LOUISA: It's a "intent" to marry.

DELL: Oh, yeah?
(Dell takes back the parchment.)

Same thing, ain't it?

LOUISA: A couple's got forty-eight hours cooling off ... or sobering up in this case ... before they can go and get hitched up. (Short pause) Besides, that thing was sealed in Michigan. We weren't in Michigan last night.

DELL: You sure of that? (Short pause) No? Gee whiz, won't my mother be so proud of me.

LOUISA: Don't you fool with me, Mr. Man.

DELL: Please, please, you can call me "Dell," Louisa. Louisa ...

LOUISA: Well, you can forget you ever heard the name. I got to get myself home before midnight tonight.

DELL: How come? You going to turn into a pumpkin? (Short pause) Where's home?

LOUISA: That's none of your darn business.

DELL: Hey, now. You don't have to get mean on me. (Short pause) I just thought we ought to get to know each other a little bit. Considering the circumstances ...

LOUISA: You're a nutso, a doughnut.

DELL: Could be ... could be.
(Dell folds the parchment and puts it into his pants pocket.)

LOUISA: What you think you're doing with that "intent"?

DELL: You want it?

LOUISA: Hell no.

DELL: Then I'll keep it.

LOUISA: What the hell for?

DELL: I don't know ... souvenir of Toledo, Ohio ... something to ease the pain of my old age ...

LOUISA: You are nuts.

DELL: Naw, I ain't nuts. Come on. I ain't nuts.

LOUISA: Yeah, you ain't nuts. You're crazy. The craziest, son of a bee sideman I ever balled.

DELL: Suppose you ball them all.

LOUISA: I get around.

DELL: I bet you do.

LOUISA: In the daytime, I'm just a spook, but in the nighttime I don't rattle chains, I swing my butt. Friday nights, I'm a soft pudding in search of a picnic.

DELL: Where you from? Bowling Green? Lima? Some small town, or a farm-girl. You must of worked in a munitions factory during the war. Must of had a soldier-boy sweetheart.

LOUISA: Bullshit.

DELL: But what happened? What happened to him? (Short pause) You're not married, are you?

LOUISA: You're spitting into the wind, Trombone Man. All your barking is up an empty tree, and the coon's done crossed the county line. Your bone-rack dogs will never catch him.

DELL: Him? (Short pause) You sure I lost the scent?

LOUISA: If I had anything going for me, if I was looking for anything

more than a piece of ass, I'd go to church or something. I sure would-
n't go and get picked up by a sideman at a dance. I got a couple more
brains than you figure.

DELL: Is that a fact?

LOUISA: Look, we did some balling, some goofing around. That's what
I come to this town looking for, besides some shopping and some
dancing, and that's what I got. Up to now anyways. I got my secrets,
my own little hell. You got no right to grill me like a slab of side bacon.

DELL: (wildly) Side bacon!
        (Dell slaps his hands. He moves about, quickly, scratching his
        head, slapping his hands.)
Bacon, bacon, bacon. What's bacon got to do with it? Right! Slab! At
the dance the other night you were with a big guy, a big, big guy, you
were dancing.

LOUISA: I like em big, I like em small. I like to swing, I like to ball.

DELL: Yeah, yeah, but this was a big, big guy, and you were with him
through the whole second set. You seemed to know each other pretty
good. I had my eye on you by the second set. The second set! I'm back
to the second set. Oh, my head doesn't like this excitement. (Short
pause) Louisa, you got to remember him.

LOUISA: A big, big guy?
        (Dell spreads his arms out wide, puffs out his belly and holds
        his breath.)

DELL: Right.

LOUISA: Big turnipy nose?

DELL: Yeah.

LOUISA: Little beady pig eyes?

DELL: Okay, okay.

LOUISA: Passed out and snored so loud the band had to fake it through the slow numbers?

DELL: So that's the guy!

LOUISA: Just before the last set, he threw up all over the drummer in the men's can.

DELL: That's him. That's him.

LOUISA: That was Yulie Moss.

DELL: (with profound joy) Yulie Moss!

LOUISA: The big, fat pig.

DELL: You know him!

LOUISA: Yeah, I know the guy. We're from the same little town. But I wasn't with him the other night. He just followed me around, that's all. What made you think of him?

DELL: Look, it's like you say "bacon," and I say "big guy," and you say "Yulie Moss," and we're already back to the second set Friday night. We got that much. (Short pause) It's like a jigsaw puzzle. We work with the pieces one at a time until we discover whole areas of color and form. Then we work with the blocks until they begin to connect with one another, and a picture of the weekend takes shape in our minds. We'll know what happened.

LOUISA: Well, you'll have to do it without this spook. I don't remember nothing. I never do.

DELL: You remembered Yulie Moss.

LOUISA: Like a ghost passing another ghost in a dream. (Laughs) Yulie

Moss. Yulie Moss and a bottle of pink slow gin.

DELL: Sloe gin ...?

LOUISA: (Still laughing) Yeah ... This weren't the other night I'm talking about, Bone Man. Don't get your hopes up. This was years ago at
a little county fair. (Short pause) The last night of the fair, the last couple taking the last ride on the ferris wheel, and Yulie and me were
looking for a haystack behind the stables. A bottle of pink sloe gin
making a big bulge in his pants pocket. Ha. We was laughing and
drinking and kissing, having a pretty good time until Yulie started
working me over like a pinball machine. I couldn't move, the big, fat
pig, but the first chance I got, I clamped my teeth down hard as I could
on Yulie's nose. I had his blower better than a rat's ass in a mousetrap.
He was dancing, screaming to beat the band, his wing-ding naked as
you please by the light of the moon, straight as a shovel handle, swinging around like a water witcher's stick gone plumb loco. (Short pause)
Hah. But he let go of me. He didn't want to wrestle no more.
      (Pause)
Back home, folks call me a bad girl, guess what you'd call a black
sheep, you know. But how half-assed wrong can a people be? Oh, I'm
a girl all right, but a good girl, a good-time summer girl who likes a
good time, and I do what I have to to get it. I got to move, I got to keep
moving. Damn what people decide to think of me. And the same goes
for you, Mr. Trombone Man. And every other son of a bitch that's
ever tried to put a handle on me. Put me where they want. (Short
pause) Every man I've ever known has tried to hold me down, has
scared me half to death.
      (Louisa moves away from Dell.)
My dad was the meanest man on earth. I was held down real hard.
(Short pause) But my brother, the baseballer, was the one who scared
me the most. (Short pause) One day, Chester had no one to catch him,
so he takes me out behind the barn and hands me a catcher's mitt. I
was ten years old. He tells me to hold the mitt out in front of me, and
don't move. Don't move, he says, not one inch, or you'll swallow the
damn ball. Now, my big brother was a god to me then ... a seventeen
year-old god in overalls throwing a ninety mile an hour fastball. Zing.

Pop. Zing. Pop. Zing. My hand swole up like a small mush melon, but he never hit me once. I never moved. Never swallowed the damn ball. I was too scared to move. Too dumb scared to move.

(Pause)

I ain't no regular bandchick, you see. I don't ball every trombone that comes walking into the Toledo bus station.

DELL: You're nobody's kewpie doll. And you ain't your everyday star-fucker neither. I know who and what I am pretty good, and I know what it adds up to. I'm a fourth-chair trombone in a third-rate band. I got a two-dollar room for one night only. The night's been had. Zero. (Short pause) Only, only I got two good hands, and just one of them wants to take hold of the door knob so I can walk out of here. My other hand is quivering at my side like a bird in troubled sleep. It wants to wake and fly straight ahead for you. (Short pause) Ha, ain't that the sweetest thing you heard today?

LOUISA: Any more sugar, I'll swear you got a honey pot for a mouth. (Short pause) It's too hot for sugar, honey. Just toss me a towel. I got to warsh my face and get out of this hotel room. Don't try and scratch my back like a pussy cat. Just toss me a towel. I got to move.

(Dell picks up a towel and throws it across the room. Louisa catches it with a quick snap of her hand. She washes her face. Takes her time. Dries off with the towel.)

Maybe I can warsh this heat-box town off my face, then you can fly whatever you got a quivering all over me again. (Short pause) I been your lady for two nights and a day, so another toss in the sack don't matter much. Just keep in mind I got a bus to catch.

(Dell looks at Louisa. Louisa looks at him.)

DELL: I don't want no more balling jazz, lady. I got my share of one-nighters. I can have a different-colored pussy every night. I've slept with a sexual circus, I've slept with a nun. I've had your sweet body next to me all weekend. I just want some talk with somebody. I like you. I like your style. You're trying to be someone who lives above the timberline where nothing grows, but Ohio's nothing more than rolling hills, and you're an Ohio girl. (Short pause) It's real simple, Louisa. I think you're somebody I can talk to.

LOUISA: Talk then, ha, talk all you want. But you'll have to talk while I'm getting.

> (Louisa moves across the room and begins picking up her things, but Dell doesn't move.)

Ain't you got a bus waiting, too, Mr. One-nighter?

DELL: Naw, ain't no bus waiting for me. Not anymore. A couple of hours ago there was a bus for me to catch, but it was two hundred miles away from here.

LOUISA: Well, what you doing then? You'll lose your job.

DELL: I guess I quit the band.

LOUISA: You're giving up your bone?

DELL: Yeah, I'm calling it a career. I've had enough of the road.

LOUISA: You're crazy.

DELL: You already told me that.

LOUISA: Now I know you're crazy.

DELL: Because I'm hanging it up?

LOUISA: Nutso.

DELL: Nutso?

LOUISA: What are you doing it for?

DELL: The road. The food. The booze. Waking up on the bus to somebody's dirty socks in my face. Waking up to a hotfoot. Waking up drunk and sick and lonely. You name it.

LOUISA: But you got a talent to look after.

DELL: Look, I ain't Jack Jenney, or Dorsey even. I got a pedestrian talent, that's all.

LOUISA: What's that mean?

DELL: I sound okay at a private party and worse in public.

LOUISA: You're full of bull.

DELL: First, I'm crazy ... now, I'm full of bull.

LOUISA: You're throwing it all away.

DELL: I ain't throwing nothing away.

LOUISA: What are you going to do? Get a job in a factory?

DELL: We live in a free society, don't we? Everybody has got the same choice ... get a job or be a bum. If I have to, I have to. I got to eat.

LOUISA: Nutso, nutso.

DELL: How you figure?

LOUISA: You got a talent, Trombone Man. You got something not many people got. Now, don't you throw your hands up in the air. A jazz man's got it easy compared to your average Joe. You can say to hell with the real world. You got a good time all the time. You got plenty of dough, plenty of dames. You got the world on a string. Yeah, sitting on a rainbow. You know what it's like down there on the street without a talent? You know the kind of crap most people got to eat down there? (Short pause) But you ... you still got a choice. You got ... Whatcha looking at me like that for? You just think I'm dumb.

DELL: You ain't so dumb.

LOUISA: Well, thank you, Mr. Bone Man. No, I ain't so dumb. Just dumb, stupid luck is all. You want to know how I go about rubbing two cents together? You want to know that?

DELL: Okay.

LOUISA: I scrub out toilets for a living. I'm working with the wrong end of a mop eight hours a day. I'm on my hands and knees cutting gobs of gum with a paint scraper. I scrape shit off of walls. Nigger work in a nowhere town. Maybe I'll get on an assembly line someday. Get to know some other girls. I got my name in at Ford. (Short pause) Or maybe I'll lose my job. Maybe I'll lose the only thing I got.
       (She is almost crying.)

DELL: Louisa.
       (Dell moves to comfort Louisa, but she turns away from him.)

LOUISA: It's okay, Bone Man. I'm okay. I ...

DELL: Did I say something wrong?

LOUISA: No, no ... How could you say something wrong when I been doing the talking for both of us? (Short pause) Just like me too, I guess, to hog the show when somebody else wants to talk. (Short pause) Sorry, Mr. Bone. I'm real sorry.

DELL: For what?

LOUISA: Sorry I called you all those names. Sorry I didn't give you a word in edgewise when you was so sweet in wanting to have a talk with me. Well, I still got two elbows ... go ahead and bend them for me. If your talking is as good as your loving, it'll be interesting.

DELL: Hey, now, I ain't no travelling preacher looking for a soapbox.

LOUISA: Nobody said you was. You ain't no preacher when you're making love to a girl. If talk is what settles you out, I'm finally giving you a chance. (Short pause) Just do me one little favor since I'm being so nice to you all of a sudden.

DELL: Yeah ...?

LOUISA: Take a match to that piece of paper you got in your pocket.

DELL: The license?

LOUISA: The "intent".

DELL: The same thing.

LOUISA: It is not!

DELL: Hey, what's eating you now, Louisa?

LOUISA: You got a hold on me. I won't let no man have a hold on me.

DELL: What hold on you?

LOUISA: All right, so it's just a big joke to you. Something to laugh about over your whisky on the bus. A belly laugh with the boys passing it around for all of them to take a look and laugh at me.

DELL: I wouldn't laugh at your expense. I never would.

LOUISA: You got no right to keep a hold on that "intent".

DELL: Why not?

LOUISA: Because it's something between the both of us, that's why not. I got a right to see it burned up, to see your hold on me nothing but ashes.

DELL: I thought you didn't want nothing to do with it.
        (Dell takes the parchment from his pocket and unfolds it into
        his hands. He looks at it and whistles.)
Gee, we must have been two drunks too long to have ... (Whistles

again) When I think about it, I swear I'll never drink again. Then, when I think about it some more, I swear I need another drink. (Short pause) One thing though, I think this is a real tender document. I guess I just wanted to look at it again sometime. Wow. Our signatures are really jumping. We must have been swinging.

> (Dell moves to the bedside table, takes a Zippo lighter from his pants pocket, looks at the parchment. Pause. Dell ignites the parchment with the lighter and drops the burning paper into the ashtray. He watches it burn.)

Louisa, I'll play any song you want to hear. We had ourselves one good, straight ahead time. I don't want it to get messed up.

LOUISA: Okay.

> (Dell notices the Bible beside the ashtray and picks it up.)

DELL: Hey, what's this doing out?

> (Louisa shrugs her shoulders.)

(reading) "How fair is thy love, my sister, my spouse; how much better is thy love than wine! and the smell of thine ointments than all spices! Thy lips, O my spouse, drop as the honeycomb: honey and milk are under thy tongue; and the smell of thy garments is like the smell of Lebanon."

LOUISA: (from memory) "A garden inclosed is my sister, my spouse; a spring shut up, a fountain sealed." (Short pause) *The Song of Solomon*, chapter four, verses ten, eleven ... and twelve. (Short pause) I know it ... by heart. It's my favorite book in the Bible.

DELL: Oh ...?

LOUISA: What's wrong with that?

DELL: Nothing, nothing. It's beautiful. (Short pause) I never got much education that way. Were we reading the Bible last night?

LOUISA: Who cares?

> (Long pause. Louisa moves to the bed and begins to collect her articles of clothing. She picks up her stockings from the

114

floor, smooths her dress, looks about for her shoes. Dell wants to say something, but he doesn't know what to say. He returns the Bible to the table and looks again at Louisa.)

DELL: Yeah ... I guess we may as well check out of here.

LOUISA: Suit yourself. I know I got to get.

(Pause. Louisa is busy. Dell moves hopelessly about the room.)
DELL: How many times does it happen in your life? When you know you're in the groove like we must have known it last night? Like a big band that's really into the music. It don't happen as often as some people like to think. Wow! Those few nights, damn few nights when the band's so together from the first note they hit to the last drum solo. A mob of kids shaking the rafters and rocking the foundations through half a dozen forty minute sets. The band so strong, so great. That's life. That's it. Beautiful.

LOUISA: That's it, Bone Man. (Short pause) Only it's two days later now. The janitor's folded all the chairs and gone home for the weekend to his wife and kids. The dancefloor's swept and cold. The band's on the road.

DELL: Yeah ... (Short pause) You know, when I was a kid, I hit it all the time. Growing up, I had two passions that tore through my body like fire. Blowing my bone ... and running ... and not necessarily in that order. Running all the time. Just running, wherever I went. (Short pause) When I was seventeen, I didn't believe ... I absolutely refused to believe anyone could outrun me in a foot race. And I run them all. Hundred yards was my piece of cake. And the four-forty. And the eight-eighty. And the mile and cross country. Running, running, sometimes three, four track meets a week.
(Pause. Louisa moves away from Dell. Goes to her overnight bag and begins to pack it neatly. Dell moves to the bed, looks at the trombone for a moment.)
Boy, was I ever surprised the first time anyone went around me in a foot race. How could anyone run that fast? I don't mean against the clock. I didn't believe anyone could go around me because I always gave it the best I

had. (Short pause) But it happened, it had to happen. In the state finals, a guy from East Chicago got the jump on me, and it didn't matter if we were two bullets or two turtles, I couldn't run as fast as he could.

(Pause)

But I kept on running, running ... through school, through jobs, cars, women. Hitting that top note when I could.

(Pause. Louisa turns away from Dell. She looks into the mirror at the vanity. She applies lipstick to her mouth. Then she touches each cheek with her lipstick, rubs it in with her fore finger and applies a bit of powder to her cheeks to make a rouge. Dell picks up the trombone case and puts it on the bed. He begins to disassemble the trombone.)

Even in the army, I was running. You got it, a courier. I flew all over the Pacific Theatre ... Hawaii, the Fiji Islands, New Guinea. Name the place, I was there like a hot potato with guns up my ass.

(Dell snaps open the trombone case and begins to clean and pack his instrument. He does this methodically.)

Believe it, a three-day pass in paradise was a solo I could handle. Whole days laying on a sand beach fishing with a hand line in the surf.

(Pause. Dell closes the trombone case. Louisa is packing her brush, comb, lipstick and powder into her purse and closes it.)

There was a great little hotel outside of Suva in the Fijis run by this old guy, an American, who claimed he'd been shipwrecked on the islands for forty years. Talk about bullshit. You needed a truck to haul his ... away. (Short pause) Yeah. Wow. Louisa ...

(Pause. Louisa turns away form the vanity and looks at Dell.)

This old guy took a shine to me and one night invited me up to his rooms for some twenty year-old whisky. Told me stories all night long. Said he worked for Pony Express as a stable boy, panned gold in the Yukon, worked the copper mines of Bolivia for ten cents a day. (Short pause) What he admired the most on the surface of the earth was the Great Coral Reef made up of tiny animals' skeletons over millions and millions of years. He said mankind could burn in Hitler's inferno or live to harvest the stars. (Short pause) We're blind dancers. We'll never do anything as pure or beautiful as that white bar of wonder.

(Pause)

Bill ... that was his name ... Bill claimed he hit it big diving for pearls.

Enough pearls to keep himself in banknotes for ... how'd he put it ... until the buzzards picked his bones. (Short pause) Oh, the pearls were probably just more of his bull, but I didn't care. His whisky was good and his company better. I sat there grinning from ear to ear until the sun come up from the Pacific and pushed the stars one by one from the sky. He said the sun was the perfect pearl. (Short pause) And it was strange ... the sea blue-white, a flat calm, and I imagined it wasn't water at all but the surface of a seashell with a pearl of the sky in its palm.

(Pause. Dell and Louisa float through it.)

Louisa ... (Short pause) You know what? Bill was telling me the truth. His bullshit was not bullshit. He showed them to me. Yeah. He took down a wooden box from the mantle of his bookshelf and showed me all his pearls.

(Pause. For a moment, Dell and Louisa look at each other without moving.)

LOUISA: That's a real purty story, Trombone Man. You got me all goose-bumpy with your South Sea stories, and when I make a move, I'm walking into someone else's dream where everything's so strange, and so fine.

(Pause. Louisa moves to the centre of the room. She's about to dance.)

I can really swing with you. I feel so fine. So strange. I'm scared. How you get to hold me so fine and strange? I feel like I knowed you all my life. I never saw you before. Two nights from now, you won't remember the color of my dress or my eyes or my hair. And that's the way I want it to be.

(Pause. Louisa dances.)

If you take me for a dumb chick, a dumb chick in a dumb town, you're all right about me. So fine. So strange. (Short pause) Now, I'm dumb about sidemen, too, I reckon. I was beginning to figure I was pretty smart about them. Best kind of man for a good-time girl. Get me a sideman for a one-night stand. If they're off the road for a day, they'll take you out for ham and eggs. If they've a bus to catch, there'll be a five-dollar bill in the toe of your shoe. (Short pause) There's my dreams, Mr. Bone. Hah, I'm back walking already in my own dreams. Pretty cheap, huh? A pretty cheap dream.

DELL: I don't believe that, Louisa.

LOUISA: (laughs) It ain't cheap to you, huh?

DELL: It ain't your dream.

LOUISA: You don't know nothing about it. I just walked in your dream a little while. Thank God you never stepped in mine. (Short pause) It's time to go. All the spooks are walking on by.
(Pause. Louisa goes and picks up her things.)
All I want to do is wake up someday and forget every day of my life. Don't try to take a hold of me. Oh. I swear you'll hit me like a twister ... I can't let go.

DELL: You got no hold on anything because you're above the timberline again where nothing grows. You're up there all by your lonesome. Hey, Louisa. Hello! Hello up there. (Short pause) You can't even hear me. (Short pause) You want to go for breakfast? I'll buy you ham and eggs, toast and marmalade. You want a five-dollar bill?
(Dell pulls a couple of bills from his pocket and tosses them on the bed.)
I got a fifty to stuff your shoe. I got a second-hand trombone. It'll hock for three or four ten-spots.
(Dell grabs his tuxedo jacket, throws it on the bed.)
The tux will bring you another twenty. I'll fill your shoe, you won't be able to get it through the door. Just come down. Come down where things can grow. (Short pause) Maybe you ended up on a cheap weekend with a drunken sideman, but that don't make it your dream. I think we got the same dream, Louisa.

LOUISA: What's that?

DELL: It's got to do with somebody we can go to and talk to, get some direction or understanding or sympathy ... whatever it is people need out of each other. But you got to come down. You got to turn around.

LOUISA: I can't turn around. I won't. I can't. (Short pause) You opened it up a little bit. A whole world. (Short pause) If you hear of anything new, be sure and let me know. I want to try it.

DELL: Louisa! We weren't in Michigan last night. There wasn't no J.P. We never left this room. (Short pause) The license ... the "intent" ... was just a fake.

LOUISA: Fake ...?

DELL: One of the guys in the band got them from his old man who's a J.P., and he gave them to everybody for a joke. He said it'd come in handy someday if a bandchick with a lot of dough ... (Short pause) I carried mine in the trombone case because it's the only thing I get up to day after day, dream after dream. Last night, we filled it in.

LOUISA: It was all make believe.

DELL: No. We filled it in.

LOUISA: A big phoney joke, and you got a kick out of seeing me all hopped up.

DELL: It wasn't a joke!

LOUISA: (laughs aloud) It was a dream.

DELL: Yeah, a dream. A dream. Louisa, let's stop running, if only for one moment. Last night, we traded vows. Blind dancers. We did it.

LOUISA: Don't ever give it up. Don't ever quit. Whatever it is you want to do. (Short pause) I know we did it. (Short pause) Dell. (Short pause) I knew it all the time.
        (They look at each other. They smile. Lights.)

END OF PLAY